Praise for *Dig Your Heels In*

"Joan Kuhl has proven to be an unabashed champion for girls' leadership and advancing women in the workplace. *Dig Your Heels In* is a solid playbook that arms women with real-world strategies for disrupting the corporate world and getting what we deserve."
—**Sophia Amoruso, cofounder and CEO, Girlboss**

"An incredibly important book that will change the way we lead, grow, and transform our organizations—and ourselves. *Dig Your Heels In* distills the essence of what it takes to become a significant change agent, guiding us to challenge the status quo and moving us from where we are to where we are called to be."
—**Frances Hesselbein, Chairman, Frances Hesselbein Leadership Forum; Presidential Medal of Freedom recipient; and former CEO, Girl Scouts of the USA**

"Need a dose of inspiration and career strategy before your next mansplaining? Here it is! As much as *Lean In* charted the course, *Dig Your Heels In* is about staying the course. A very special message to millennial women that will take them through, not just to, the glass ceiling. The stories in this book are as inspiring as they are instructive. "Joan Kuhl was among the first thought leaders to focus intently on young leaders and by doing so has inspired me to a lifetime of developing millennials before they assume top leader roles. A profoundly talented writer and speaker, Joan is a standard bearer for women in business. *Dig Your Heels In* is not just about standing firm; it's about moving ahead."
—**Tom Kolditz, PhD, retired Brigadier General and Executive Director, The Doerr Institute for New Leaders, Rice University**

"Our girls need advocates like Joan Kuhl to help them grow up to be strong, respected, and valued leaders. *Dig Your Heels In* emphasizes the bold moves that individuals can take to ensure women of all ages, levels, and backgrounds have the time, space, and support to be our authentic selves in a world of social pressures and gender stereotypes."
—**Kate T. Parker, photographer and author of *Strong Is the New Pretty***

"Women face specific challenges to rise in their careers and oftentimes shrink themselves at the prospect of engaging others around their ambitions. *Dig Your Heels In* gives women permission and courage to go after what they need and deserve while also strengthening their peer network to empower women around them."

—**Sally Helgesen, coauthor of** *How Women Rise*

"Women deserve to know the real deal so they can power through the obstacles that they will encounter in pursuit of the happy, fulfilling, and successful careers they deserve. *Dig Your Heels In* is a movement based on having the courage to advocate for ourselves and play the long game for our peers and the women to follow."

—**Annie McKee, author of** *How to be Happy at Work* **and Senior Fellow, University of Pennsylvania**

"*Dig Your Heels In* delivers relevant and actionable strategies to empower women to lead within their organizations."

—**Anne Ackerley, Head of BlackRock's US and Canada Defined Contribution Group and Cofounder of BlackRock's Women's Initiative Network**

"Practical solutions, relevant stories, and even scripts for difficult situations make *Dig Your Heels In* a must-read for any woman who wants to advance her career and change her organization for the better."

—**Laura Vanderkam, author of** *I Know How She Does It*

"The trust and influence that Joan Kuhl has earned through her research-based consulting projects and passion for transforming culture are infectious. We have worked together for the past several years on efforts to engage early career professionals and advance women in sports, so I'm thrilled that her advice and strategies are accessible through her new book, *Dig Your Heels In*, to more leaders in human resources and talent management."

—**Holly Lindvall, Senior Vice President, Human Resources & Diversity, New York Mets**

"For over a decade, I have witnessed Joan Kuhl's impact on global organizations and diverse leaders led by her passion for early career development and advancement of women in the workplace. *Dig Your Heels In* pulls together Joan's expertise with inspiring stories of trailblazers who provide a realistic pathway for achieving success at work and in life."

—**Marshall Goldsmith, #1** *New York Times* **bestselling author of** *Triggers*, *Mojo*, **and** *What Got You Here Won't Get You There* **and #1 Executive Coach and the only two-time #1 Leadership Thinker in the World, Thinkers50**

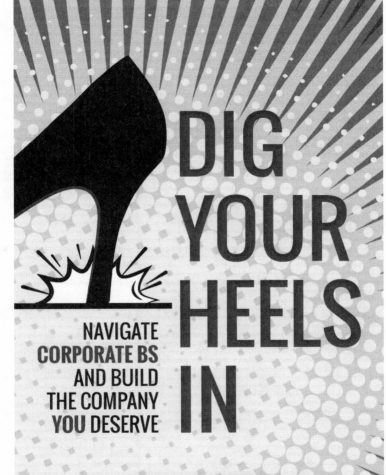

DIG YOUR HEELS IN

NAVIGATE CORPORATE BS AND BUILD THE COMPANY YOU DESERVE

JOAN KUHL

BK

Berrett–Koehler Publishers, Inc.

Copyright © 2019 by Joan Kuhl

Berrett-Koehler Publishers, Inc.
1333 Broadway, Suite 1000
Oakland, CA 94612-1921
Tel: (510) 817-2277   Fax: (510) 817-2278   www.bkconnection.com

Ordering Information
Quantity sales. Special discounts are available on quantity purchases by corporations, associations, and others. For details, contact the "Special Sales Department" at the Berrett-Koehler address above.

Individual sales. Berrett-Koehler publications are available through most bookstores. They can also be ordered directly from Berrett-Koehler: Tel: (800) 929-2929; Fax: (802) 864-7626; www.bkconnection.com

Orders for college textbook/course adoption use. Please contact Berrett-Koehler: Tel: (800) 929-2929; Fax: (802) 864-7626.

Distributed to the U.S. trade and internationally by Penguin Random House Publisher Services.

Berrett-Koehler and the BK logo are registered trademarks of Berrett-Koehler Publishers, Inc.

Printed in the United States of America

Berrett-Koehler books are printed on long-lasting acid-free paper. When it is available, we choose paper that has been manufactured by environmentally responsible processes. These may include using trees grown in sustainable forests, incorporating recycled paper, minimizing chlorine in bleaching, or recycling the energy produced at the paper mill.

Cataloging-in-Publication Data

Names: Kuhl, Joan Snyder, author.
Title: Dig your heels in : navigate corporate bs and build the company you
    deserve / Joan Kuhl.
Description: First Edition. | Oakland, CA : Berrett-Koehler Publishers, 2019.
Identifiers: LCCN 2018048877 | ISBN 9781523098354 (paperback)
Subjects: LCSH: Women—Employment. | Career development—Case studies. |
    Women—Social networks. | BISAC: BUSINESS & ECONOMICS / Workplace
    Culture. | BUSINESS & ECONOMICS / Careers / General.
Classification: LCC HD6053 .K84 2019 | DDC 331.4—dc23
LC record available at https://lccn.loc.gov/2018048877

FIRST EDITION

25 24 23 22 21 20 19   10 9 8 7 6 5 4 3 2 1

Production manager: Susan Geraghty
Cover design: Susan Malikowski, DesignLeaf Studio, and Florence Lee,
        Why Millennials Matter
Interior design and composition: Westchester Publishing Services
Copyeditor: Michele D. Jones
Proofreader: Sophia Ho
Indexer: Sylvia Coates
Author photo: Wendy Yalom

Contents

Chapter Action Summaries   *181*

This book is dedicated to my daughters,
Addison and Juliette.

Dream with your full imagination, hold your ground,
and go after everything you want and deserve.

Introduction

Thriving, Not Just Surviving

Imagine the effort it must take to wake up every morning with the daunting task of walking into an environment that tests your beliefs about who you can and could be as well as what you truly deserve. Have you ever looked around in disbelief as you observe how much bias shows up in decisions and actions with outcomes that are just not right? Is it that hard to believe that millions of women of all ages feel like this every day? They struggle to move up the ladder or gain fulfillment in their day-to-day work. Some feel underpaid and underappreciated, but it's not just a feeling; it is proven fact. In 2018, women still earned 77 cents for every male dollar over their lifetimes; parity between the sexes begins to drop the minute a woman chooses to have kids, and it never recovers. By the time a woman reaches the age of fifty, she's earning 55 cents on the dollar compared to her male counterpart.[1]

Even our youngest generation in the workplace, millennial women between eighteen and thirty-seven in 2018, say they feel that their gender has held them back in their careers.[2]

Some feel harassed or that they need to compromise their values because they are paralyzed by fear of retaliation. In fact, 20 percent of millennial women "strongly agree" that women are less likely to be considered for senior-level roles in a business or corporate setting than their male counterparts,[3] and over 40 percent of working women have been the victim of sexism in the workplace.[4] Companies that these women had perceived as places where they could grow and advance their careers are deeply disappointing to them.

I remember the first time a customer grabbed me inappropriately in his office, in front of his secretary. I jumped and called out while he just laughed and walked away. And I can't forget the moment when another customer tried to humiliate me about a topic related to our business in front of a huge room of people by taunting me about my looks and intelligence. I was twenty-one years old. That night, I memorized a ten-page study regarding the treatment of schizophrenia (which I can still recite to this day) and marched into his office the next morning to show him I knew my stuff. I wasted so much energy feeling belittled in similar situations, without any outlet for support.

Over time, women's frustration in dealing with subtle and overt sexism paired with a lack of advancement opportunities and an unsupportive corporate culture is too much to bear. That is why millennial women are quitting in record numbers to embark on the adventure of "doing their 'own thing.'" They are transferring their energy and passion, derived in many cases from a side hustle, into a full-time entrepreneurial focus. But this self-starter option, though glorified by social media, is not for everyone.

Women at the height of their career are also moving on to bigger and better opportunities outside their current organizations because they can't hold the umbrella any longer. It's becoming way too heavy as they try to be a positive North Star for the next generation while continuing to operate at senior leadership levels as "the only woman." It's lonely at the top, and they also still lack the systemic support needed to transform their company. The costs to their personal lives in having to navigate a male-dominated, monolithic, conservative culture are exhausting. They are as desperate for change as the youngest, most junior women in the workforce.

Some women remain in their corporate jobs because of the time invested or the burden of student loan debt. Others have convinced themselves that things may get better and that the benefits to come are worth the stifling of their true feelings. But in assuming either stance and accepting the status quo, they are surrendering their ambitions and simply going through the motions.

Does this sound like you? Armed with the "Lean In" battle cry, you embarked on your career with greater confidence and higher expectations than did women of previous generations. But you soon discovered that your passion and excitement were quelled under the compounding pressure to behave like a "good girl." You are struggling to find your voice despite your desire to question, challenge, or hold leadership accountable for more equitable conditions.

Faced with these conflicting forces, you are considering giving up on your professional aspirations and walking away from the very company whose door you worked so hard to get through.

So what can you do if you're feeling discouraged and wondering whether leaving is your only (less than ideal) option? How can you navigate through companies whose bad behaviors and systemic challenges were in place over a hundred years ago?

If this is you, I believe you are in a unique position to make your voice—and our collective voice as women—matter . . . by digging your heels in.

Dig Your Heels In

Sheryl Sandberg's *Lean In* launched a visible and active conversation on gender bias, and the women in my own Lean In Circle have helped me push forward to make some of the boldest moves in my career. What *Dig Your Heels In* is offering is a unique perspective for the next era of change, one that builds on the success of *Lean In* and the many other women empowerment initiatives that have arisen since its launch. But it is also a double click on the systemic changes and processes we need to disrupt within the companies we work for. Changing how we approach our personal goals—and transforming companies to do better by all of us—should not be a burden resting solely on our shoulders but rather a shared mission for men and women.

As talented and valuable as you are, you *could* secure a better title, more responsibility, and more money if you leave today. But, with your relationship currency, enterprise knowledge, and track record of results, you could also cultivate the career you desire right where you are by staying and building the company you deserve. I wrote this book because I want you to hold your ground at your company, stay put, and focus on the long game. I want you to commit to transforming the place that pays your paycheck today.

Sure, you as an individual could take the other route. For some women, maybe enough is enough, and they should leave. (And I wholeheartedly support them and hope this book serves as a mirror with which to evaluate this decision.) But women collectively will not get where we all need to be if we don't make a stand together to drive the necessary changes. We need women at all levels of their professions as well as the men they work with to elevate equality as an urgent priority. Everyone employed today and in the future deserves to work for a company that is fair in pay and opportunity to both genders. Equality is good for people, good for business, and good for society.

An important note here: My goal in this book is not to convince women in toxic work situations to "grin and bear it" for the greater good. If you are facing discrimination or harassment that is eating away at your soul, your only job is to do what's best for you in your individual situation. Digging your heels in is a personal decision and is not for everybody. But for those for whom it may be the right option, consider this: The more time you spend at one particular organization, the more valuable your perspective, the more you know how it operates and who is calling the shots, and the more power you have to identify where and how to make change happen. This is how we evolve outdated, inequitable practices that reward the wrong behaviors and stifle the right ones—with you blazing the trail, creating the company that you and all the women behind you want to work for. A place that honors the right people and enforces the just practices that will ensure its success and yours over the long term. This is what happens when you dig your heels in.

What Digging Your Heels In Means to Me

I have always believed that investing time in our youngest employees should be core to every business. That's why I launched Why Millennials Matter, which helps companies understand, engage, and retain the next generation of global workers and consumers. Since an early age, I had always been enrolled in youth leadership programs across Philadelphia and the Lehigh Valley in Pennsylvania. Those experiences shaped my values and developed my confidence in pursuing leadership in my personal and professional life.

During my thirteen-year corporate career, I stayed actively involved on college campuses as a speaker, mentor, and career coach, so I knew firsthand how much power and potential this next generation possessed. But soon after the global recession, I watched companies pull back on the investments—in internship programs, leadership development opportunities, global rotations, and apprenticeship models—that engage and develop early-career professionals and expose them to new pathways and people who can be mentors and role models. I had two options. The first was to stay and accept as my new reality the challenges we faced as leaders managing more responsibility with fewer and fewer resources. Or I could do something unconventional—serve as an ally to both sides: early-career talent and the companies who need them in their workforce.

The biggest questions on my mind were, "How can I gain access to the broadest and most diverse groups of students? Who relies on recruiting off campus and needs to evolve to be the company most desired by millennials and generations to follow?" And finally, "How do I get the word out to change the message that millennials are entitled, lazy, and unworthy of investment to one that is more accurate and encouraging?" This is why I launched my company with several key clients and partners, including Barnes and Noble College, which managed over 750 college bookstores where I could be connected as their career expert and research partner to millions of students; Eli Lilly and Company; Goldman Sachs; the New York Mets, who were struggling to retain young professionals as fast as they recruited them; and *Cosmopolitan* magazine, the number-one magazine globally for millennials.

We've had some incredible assignments that have given me and my team tremendous insight across diverse industries, including health care, finance, retail, higher education, and sports. We have had the opportunity to be involved in a wide range of projects, including a multilevel generation-, gender-, and race-based engagement and retention strategy for a US pharmaceutical giant; a global HR culture initiative for both a leading media organization and one of the most prestigious investment banks; a comprehensive research, training, and talent strategy for a national retailer; a culture- and leadership-focused initiative in the sports industry; and an executive leadership development program for a major consumer goods company. We have partnered with organizations and executives who shared our mission of leading positive culture change and empowering the next-generation workforce to achieve their potential.

The engagement that had the greatest impact on me was a transformative project for Eli Lilly and Company (Lilly) called the Women's Employee Journey. This 2015 research initiative[5] explored the factors contributing to the decline in representation of women at senior levels of leadership and to better understand their overall experience as employees. It was a journey involving hundreds of women around the globe who participated in a series of focus groups to share their experiences at Lilly. As the project lead for the external research team, I conducted interviews with the executive committee and key senior leaders to frame and understand the company's top priorities and culture. Carolyn Buck Luce, a retired partner at Ernst and Young (EY) and cofounder for the Center for Talent Innovation, served as the project advisor and my mentor in working with Lilly and the Center for Talent Innovation on this research initiative.

Lilly wanted the opportunity to truly understand—through its own data and with real stories from Lilly employees—what women of all ages and levels in its workplace were experiencing. After analyzing the insights from the women across different levels and business functions, we mapped the findings back to millennial women to illustrate the impact on early-career professionals in terms of its influence on their perception about women's advancement opportunities and their personal engagement. We wanted to highlight the consequences and influence on millennial women resulting from what they were seeing and hearing from experienced women at tenured and senior levels in the company. One of the questions that continues to inform my work was the following:

Do you feel the need to change yourself to become a senior leader at your company?

In the Women's Employee Journey study, we found that the majority of female employees included in the research felt they needed to change to advance. Luckily, from the moment we presented the cumulative research findings to Lilly's executive committee, leadership was all in and firm in its commitment to move toward enterprise-wide solutions that would increase representation of women and diverse employees across all business functions.

The challenges women face are quite often systemic and controlled by leadership actions and imperatives. Enterprise-wide transformation must be a priority for CEOs and their executive committees. There is also tremendous power that can be driven by women themselves. The women's network at Lilly evolved to become a proactive movement on a mission to achieve gender parity at every level of leadership with extensive support from their CEO, Dave Ricks.

As a result, we were able to move from research to solutions by supporting Lilly's newly transformed women's network, the Women's Initiative for Leading at Lilly (WILL), and partnering with the network on several work streams in the areas of learning, development, advocacy, and advancement.

This project struck a significant chord with me personally, as Lilly was the first company I worked for out of college. I was recruited off campus and had an extraordinary experience working there for the first decade of my career. In approaching this work, I couldn't help but think about all of my friends, former colleagues, previous managers, mentors, and role models, and the leaders whom I truly respected and admired. This is also why the stories and findings haunted me for some time, compelling me to want to play a greater role in making a difference for these women and all women.

In my initial interviews with women at the executive level, I had a very naïve mind-set regarding their experiences. I had prepared my questions with excitement and awe as I memorized their resumes and imagined the allure that must surround their lifestyles, so I was emotionally unprepared to hear their pain. Each heartbreaking story of struggle to stay in the workforce through life-stage changes and battles for pay and credit was like a punch in the stomach. I admired these women, but they were not thriving in their power; they were barely surviving. Knowing the people behind the research data had a profound impact on my appreciation of the complexities and challenges in achieving equality and inclusion, and on my dedication in seeing this work through.

Yes, this work at first glance did feel like turning around the *Titanic.* But that was almost four years ago. Since then, new research has surfaced, and we have found many organizations invested in building more inclusive, equitable workplaces. Moving from research to action, I've been energized by the women and men I've worked with who are leading real-world strategies that are transforming global companies. I've also had the opportunity to experiment with my own vision for training and business initiatives that substantiate where and how women can gain traction in even the most traditional and monolithic cultures. I can't wait to share all that I've learned and connect you to the people ready to show you the way.

I have a long history of volunteering and serving on boards that support girls, such as Girls Hope of Pittsburgh, Girl Scouts of the USA, Step Up for Women, and Girls on the Run, and I'm now serving as a board member of Girls Inc. of New York City. And, more important, I am the mother of two daughters. I'm determined to do what I can because our daughters deserve a brighter future *much, much* sooner than what studies predict as our slow trajectory to equality. In many cases, "seeing is believing," and young women are judging and watching companies more closely than ever before. This is why I am determined to work with companies to help them become better.

The only way for young women and girls to achieve their dreams is to ensure that the women in the prime of their careers, like those I interviewed years ago, are thriving, *not* just surviving. We can't afford to wait the 217 years the World Economic Forum predicts it will take to achieve global workplace equality for men and women.[6] That is why I wrote this book: to empower women early in their journey to become the leaders of their companies and to make their companies the places where they thrive with their eyes wide open. I lay out the real deal about what you're up against, and I help you get ready to turn it all around in your favor.

I have been lucky to have some extraordinary mentors throughout my career journey. I had sponsors who helped me navigate my toughest decisions so that I could position myself for the success I desired personally and professionally. I want to play this role for you on a larger scale. To the women working right now who need inspiration, some air cover, empowering and practical advice, and the knowledge and know-how to move the needle in their favor, this book is dedicated to you.

In This Book

Every day there are inspiring stories of bravery and record achievements by women speaking their minds, advocating for equality, and leading transformative change across every industry. This book is for the women who likewise want to effect change and progress in their companies but are feeling de-energized and deflated, and are contemplating a way out. If they are truly going to blaze trails and make transformative change, they must dig their heels in and drive change relentlessly and collectively from the inside. It won't be easy, but the temperature has risen in the women's movement. More than ever before, today's businesses are primed for disruption and progress.

This book is your playbook for making the big moves for your career, for your company, and for all the women who will follow in your footsteps.

> In **Part One**, I will make the case for digging your heels in—why it benefits you and your career ambitions, your company, and women all over. I will discuss the pros and cons of staying and engaging versus hitting the high road, and help you make the very personal decision to dig your heels in—or not. I'll provide real-world examples of women who are finding success across different industries in diverse pathways, so that you know that it is possible.
>
> **Part Two** of this book is all about action. I will guide you through building a vision for your career at your company and making the case with the people in charge. I'll arm you with data to illustrate the real benefits to you and your business of creating a career path that works for you. I'll walk you through the big bold moves that will help you accelerate your career, ignite change, and lift up others as you climb. I will also help you tackle the common barriers women face in climbing the corporate

ladder and the self-limiting behaviors that hold us back from showing up as our authentic selves. This part of the book is also a reminder to make time in our overscheduled lives to drive this change together, to mentor, to volunteer, to speak up, to invest in the causes and organizations that support girls and diversity. We must contribute to the efforts inside and outside of work to make a brighter future for all women.

Part Three is about making work *work* with your life. You will be inspired by women's real-life tactics and examples of how to make your work worth it to you in the long run, including building the relationships that matter—to your career and your sanity!—and proven work+life hacks to make your days run more smoothly.

I've learned a great deal from hearing about the experiences of other women, whether from research or directly from friends and colleagues. That is why I've embedded throughout the book the stories of women I admire and who have taught me some of my greatest lessons. You'll meet women working for global companies such as PriceWaterhouseCoopers, BlackRock, and Eli Lilly and Company, as well as others with university and military backgrounds. They will share how they dug their heels in to build the careers and companies they deserve. I will provide you with specific, targeted advice; explicit examples; scripted responses; scenario-based strategies; and a really transparent action plan to become one of those women. When you're ready, I hope you will have the courage to share your important story, just as they have.

The World Needs Us

> **We need the collective perspective of diverse women (HER) to be represented through HER voice and for HER to leverage HER lens in which SHE sees the world, in order to innovate the products and services built by the companies where SHE works.**

Change CAN happen. I believe it, I've seen it, and I've led the charge. We've witnessed companies that are willing to change their mind-sets and cultures and adapt to the needs and wants of their employees. They are not doing this with a single online training session. They are making radical changes in how they are structured and how they communicate. They are investing in their most valuable resource: their people. And to lead these efforts, they needed women to steer and drive the solutions throughout the broadest, deepest levels of the organization. They needed women to entrench themselves and see this vision of change through by pursuing their careers to their fullest possibilities.

The very companies that have the least equitable practices are the ones that most need you to dig your heels in to create change from the inside. This may not be fair, but it's the truth—and let's be honest: this endeavor to elevate women and inspire a movement at your organization can make for one of the most rewarding professional experiences of your life.

The world needs you to **DIG YOUR HEELS IN**—for yourself and for HER.

Part 1
MAKING THE CASE

Women speaking up for themselves and for those around them is the strongest force we have to change the world.

—Melinda Gates

The Case for Digging Your Heels In (Everybody Wins)

In this chapter, you will learn how digging your heels in benefits

* Women in particular, and the world in general, by opening the doors to a new era of equality
* You, personally and professionally, by enabling you to create the career you want at the company you deserve
* The economy, by making sure women's voices are better heard and catered to in the marketplace

Women are a force in today's economy, both as employees and as consumers. Globally, we control about $20 trillion in annual consumer spending.[1] That figure could climb as high as $28 trillion in the next five years. Women make the decision in the purchase of 94 percent of home furnishings, 92 percent of vacations, 91 percent of homes, 60 percent of automobiles, and 51 percent of consumer electronics. Further, 94 percent of women are making health care decisions for themselves and others.[2] Our consumer influence touches every industry, product, and service.

We need to take control and use our influence.

Millennial women between the ages of eighteen and thirty-four are twice as likely to support brands that showcase female empowerment.[3] Say these statistics out loud. Repeat them to a friend. Bring them up at work or in casual conversations. I have included a section at the back of the book summarizing The Business Case for Change.

Women have enormous influence and power as consumers, and we are a solid force of talent in today's economy.

Despite these clear indicators of our influence, we are unable to bring our voices and unique perspectives to the forefront of the companies developing products and services to meet the demands of our global economy. We are not sitting in the front seat with the power to drive the final decisions for consumers and our workforce. What's the result? Nobody wins—not the individual woman struggling to make an impact in her workplace, not women in general, and most certainly not the economy.

The Case for Business

Women lag behind men in representation across all higher levels of leadership in almost every single industry. Although women held 51.5 percent of management, professional, and related positions, *Fortune*'s 2018 published list shows that there are only twenty-four women in Fortune 500 CEO roles.[4] This figure represents a fall of 25 percent, dropping from thirty-two in 2017, the all-time high.[5] Women are the chief executives of just 4.8 percent of the five hundred most profitable companies in the United States. Even more discouraging, according to Catalyst, women make up about 20 percent of S&P 500 board seats.[6] There are twelve Fortune 500 companies with no women on their boards whatsoever.[7]

This lack of representation in the highest positions of leadership doesn't make sense for us or for business. Research has shown that companies with three or more women on the board outperform companies with all-male boards by 60 percent on return on investment, 60 percent on return on equity, and 84 percent on return on sales.[8] In other words, a move from no women board members to 30 percent representation was associated with a 15 percent jump in profit! Yet we are not being represented and engaged at the levels where key decisions are made, and our voices continue to be stifled.

McKinsey reports that advancing women's equality could add $12 trillion to global growth by 2025.[9] This is roughly the size of the combined economies of the US and China today. Gender equality, besides being the moral choice, is an economic imperative. Our pay, our voices, our positions, our access, and our influence should be equally valued and represented. Anything less is just bad business.

As the North America head of Diabetes and Cardiovascular for Sanofi, Michelle Carnahan leads all commercial operations for the business unit in the US and Canada, which comprises Sales, Marketing, Market Access, One Trade, Innovative Solutions, and Business Operations Support. Throughout her over twenty-five-year career, she has demonstrated her skills as a passionate, patient-centric leader who consistently holds herself and the organization to high-impact results and better experiences for patients. Here is what she says about the powerful business impact of putting women in charge.

I spent a lot of time talking about the urgency for getting more women in key roles and needing to include a woman's perspective before it was fully accepted, before everyone was fully on board. As a leader in the health care industry, the power of the purse had a clear influence on our business. I did get a bit of a reputation and for a while it felt like, "Oh, there she goes again on that women thing." But what you learn when you keep pushing your point on the importance of diversity, including gender diversity, and back your voice up with enough evidence and results, through great women getting great roles then delivering solid results, it builds credibility and belief within the organization. And it really is worth it because it starts to change things, so I encourage everyone to keep pushing.

The opportunity to be a very small part of adding to a more diverse workplace and seeing that shift in a company is really exciting and highly rewarding to leaders, employees, and the bottom line.

The Case for You

I see the personal case for digging your heels in from the perspective of risk and reward. From my experiences and listening to the stories of so many women who struggled with this decision, I have concluded that the long-term reward of staying and engaging often far outweighs the risk.

Looking at the short term, it's easy to see how leaving your company for higher pay and a better title will boost your career. But what happens when you hit the wall at your new company, and, once again, you have to make the decision to dig your heels in or jump ship? How many times do you think you can go through this cycle before you burn out?

The fact is, every company has its own issues, and today almost none offer the equitable and inclusive environment women need to truly thrive. The only way for us to develop such an environment is for each of us to make the decision to create change where we are. Yes, it will be for the betterment of all women, but do you understand the magnitude of the rewards that are also in it for you?

When you decide to dig your heels in at your company, you're coming at the problem with insider knowledge. You know the pain points . . . intimately. You know the politics, you know the players, and they know you. You are uniquely positioned to make the case for change and to win. You are uniquely positioned to create exactly the type of change you need in order to attain the career you desire. You're not stepping into somebody else's plan for change and riding her or his coat tails; you are the one blazing a trail that you know will work for you.

Meanwhile, at your new company, you will have to rebuild all of your institutional knowledge and status from scratch. Why not put your energy into reaping the rewards of all the time and work you've already invested at your current company?

Another huge consideration is what being a change maker—a trailblazer—can do for your career. What do you think it does for your resume to show that you cycled through five different companies in ten years, versus crafting the career you desire, perhaps from scratch, and creating real change at one company over a longer period of time? What if you were the one who led the change to create more flexible work options, promote and retain more senior female leaders, and transform your culture to be more inclusive? What would that do to your professional status? But, perhaps more important, how would that feel?

Tiffaine Stephens, a senior marketing associate, leveraged her personal passion and commitment to diversity and inclusion to dig her heels in at a low point in her early professional career. Doing so gave her the opportunity to increase her visibility and reputation and to create real change for herself and for her personal cause.

> After my first official year at my company, I pursued an opportunity on a popular brand with a rock-star team. I seemed to have all of the right things in place: a solid resume, personal advocates, and genuine enthusiasm for my next role. What I hadn't realized at the time was that there was a sneaky thing called politics getting ready to wiggle its way into my career.

Though the decision to hire someone else was made with genuine business intent, it affected Tiffaine's engagement and where she saw herself in the company. She struggled to find a place in the organization where she could have the type of impact she was looking for. Her creativity suffered, and her overall mood at work transformed from enthusiasm to resentment.

> I was only twenty-three, with only twelve to fifteen months of associate experience, so I stayed even though I felt stuck and voiceless. It didn't help that I was a black woman in the middle of America during the prequel to November 2016. The experiences that I had outside of work were now a part of the Tiffaine I brought to work.
>
> I started to feel myself constrained by a mask. Inside I was angry about my work situation and the injustice against the black community. Outside, I smiled sweetly, nodded in agreement, and stayed enclosed. What I didn't realize then is that I was hiding the best parts of myself. The organization was not able to see what I was truly made of, and I was a part of the reason.
>
> That is when diversity and inclusion (D&I) started to become a bigger focus and passion for me. I shared these thoughts with a senior leader, and he encouraged me to leverage an existing platform to reach other associates and create a space where we could contribute to D&I.

Working in collaboration with an advisory team and leadership, Tiffaine led an all-day forum for associates across the organization. The goal was for them to champion D&I within their teams. The event drew about a hundred associates and leaders across the organization, who worked to build solutions. Tiffaine wouldn't have been able to achieve this without building relationships with people around the organization who may have had different perspectives around D&I.

> This experience did two things for me: It forced me outside of my shell and mask. It forced me to be vulnerable, and in turn I was able to demonstrate the ability to make sizable impact in a short amount of time. And it showed the organization what I was made of. My equity positively increased, which led to more opportunities.

There is a great sense of accomplishment and community that comes with digging your heels in and creating a job, company, and industry where you and other women can bring your whole selves without compromising your life priorities. This journey will unleash a much bigger and better feeling than any one-time pay raise or promotion. The ability to transform your company and your personal opportunities is life changing . . . and world changing.

The Case for the World

Our stories and our visibility shape perceptions beyond those of men and women currently in the workforce; they have the power to influence our communities and our children. When your story is one of breaking down old structures and gender biases to create a more equitable playing field, you empower other women to do the same. What is more, you lift up the next generation of girls and women to achieve more under even better working conditions.

Did you know that gender stereotypes become rigidly defined in children as young as between five and seven years of age?[10] So, even in this world where women are making every effort to lean into their careers, cheered on by mantras to be bossy and run the world, by the time women enter the professional workforce, they are carrying some hardwired biases and expectations that conflict with their ability to simply be ourselves.

In 2016, I co-led a global study for the Center for Talent Innovation focused on the motivators and career expectations of college-educated millennials who were currently employed in the workforce.[11] One of the most startling findings was when millennial women were asked, "What would you do if you were offered a senior leadership role in your company tomorrow?" they were 55 percent more likely than millennial men to turn it down!

Why is that the case? Shouldn't women feel empowered and leap toward leadership? Is this fear a result of a lack of guidance, role models, and knowledge to pioneer a demanding vision for enterprise-wide change that would allow them a fulfilling career and be their own authentic selves? Is it compounded with the overwhelming reality of imbalance in the second-shift responsibilities of child care, aging parents, and partner and personal health? If so, what can we do to change all of this? The answer is clear: Lead by example and dig your heels in.

What if kids' play houses were redesigned as doctor's and detective's offices? What if every public and school library had sections dedicated to women? What if the walls of our preschool and kindergarten classrooms were decorated with more pictures of female firefighters, female doctors, female adventurers, and female business leaders? What if you were one of those business leaders whose portrait was on the wall? What could this do for helping the next generation break through the biases that hold our generation back? **We need to start in the playroom to get more women in the board room**.

Colonel (retired) Diane Ryan is currently the associate dean for programs in administration at the Jonathan M. Tisch College for Civic Life at Tufts University. Prior to joining Tufts, Diane was an academy professor, director of the Eisenhower Leader Development Program with Columbia University, and deputy department head in the Department of Behavioral Sciences and Leadership at the United States Military Academy, West Point, New York. During her twenty-nine-year career as a US Army officer Diane served in a variety of command and staff assignments both stateside and abroad. During her last combat assignment with the 1st Cavalry Division in Baghdad, Iraq, she founded a US-Iraqi partnership for military women and worked with several NGOs on peace and security initiatives. More recently, she served as a strategy consultant to the commander of US Army Pacific designing leader development exchange programs for several key US partners. She earned a PhD in social and community psychology and has studied the impact of stereotypes on professional identity and organizational commitment. Diane was in elementary school during the height of the women's movement in the 1970s. Here is what she has to say about the power of representation:

> I remember in fourth grade writing for the school newspaper at my middle school and my very first published article was about the ratification of the Equal Rights Amendment. Clearly I understood this was a problem at the time, even though I couldn't quite wrap my head

around how it might affect me personally. In a way, I was lucky. I grew up in a rural area and, just to note, in my high school class, the women were the really high performers. All of the class officers were women as well as the valedictorians, National Merit winners, etc. I was oblivious to the fact that girls were "less than" at that time and consider myself fortunate to be somewhat sheltered during these formative years. My earliest ambition was to be a doctor and I can't remember anyone ever telling me that I could not be. A lot of that had to do with the role models around me. Both my parents worked and I was a latchkey kid from third grade on. My dad got home first and put dinner on the table every night which was quite unusual for the times but definitely created expectations for me about equal partnerships. My pediatrician was a woman named Ruth Pagano and had a huge influence on my career goals. From the age of four years old I had these women in my life who worked and made it work. In the case of my doctor, I saw myself in somebody who I aspired to be like.

Another reason why digging your heels in benefits women is the correlated effect that occurs when we increase female percentages in the executive echelons. The research shows that more women at the top strengthens the effort to attract and hire talented women at the middle and bottom of the organization as well. This means that when you dig your heels in, you're not only making it easier for the next women CEOs but also making the business world more hospitable to women at all levels—from the mailroom to the boardroom. Even if that woman in the mailroom has no desire to move up the corporate ladder and stays in the same position for the next twenty years, your creating change in the company will make her life easier and more fulfilling. Now how rewarding is that?

Your Unique Battle—and Opportunity

Women see the world differently, and it's an extraordinary perspective we should share with the world. We should be able to channel our direct and indirect experiences into the creative, operational, and analytical processes within our companies. Beginning with our own ideas as examples, we can drive the case for enterprise-wide standards for diverse, inclusive, "gender-smart," and "generation-smart" leadership and create a better world for ourselves, for business, and for women everywhere.

Digging your heels in is not an easy task, and I get that it doesn't feel fair that you have to. Women didn't create the problem of gender bias and inequality, so why should we be the ones tasked with fixing it? Simply put, it's because it will never happen otherwise.

Digging your heels in may be an uphill battle, but it is your unique crusade—and your distinct opportunity to transform from being the victim to being the solution, to make your mark, to change your company, and to change the world.

Making the Decision

In this chapter, you will
* **Learn about the factors influencing your individual decision to dig your heels in (or not)**
* **Diagnose your company culture and how and where you can begin to create change (or not)**
* **Answer DYHI reflection questions to help you decide whether to stay or to walk**
* **Explore the science, emotion, and impact of wake-up calls**

The big question you have to ask yourself in making the decision to dig your heels in or not is this: By leaving your company, are you running away from something or running toward something? Are you jumping ship because you just can't "deal" any longer, or is the new opportunity something that really excites you and fulfills your career ambitions? If it isn't, moving on may not be the right decision for you, at least not right now. And let's be clear: I want to help guide and support you so that you make that decision with higher certainty and confidence.

It is important to consider whether that opportunity on the horizon is really all that it's cracked up to be. At the very least, you are clear on the status quo in your current organization. What do you know about your new future workplace? What power will you have to eliminate the barriers and inequity you may face there? You'll be working from the starting line to build up your reputation and operational knowledge—two key factors in creating change—so it's important to know what you're lining up for.

Last, what is the opportunity cost of leaving the company in which you have already invested so many years, developed so much institutional knowledge, and built so many key relationships? How far could you get if you decided to dig your heels in instead, using that equity to create a career path that works for you and your ambitions?

For Laura Vang, the opportunity to dig her heels in at IBM Watson Health Life Sciences has accelerated her professional development, which may not have come about otherwise. She is more apt to speak her mind and bring her authentic self to the job. In addition, the act of working on change has developed her capacity and reputation as an authentic leader.

> Interestingly, advocating for my tenure at IBM has had a couple of side effects: I feel more tied to the culture and mission of this place because I speak up about it. And I can see the development ramifications: I've noticed that this is a leadership skill. There's an *individual contributor* positivity that you are the "doer" who can implement change. Separately, there's a *leadership* positivity that helps align the employees in the organization to the same mission and beliefs.

Obviously, the decision to stay or go is a very personal one, and there is no one "right" way to make it. Taking a full inventory of your situation, you may say enough is enough. If the job is taking an irreparable toll on your self-esteem, self-worth, happiness, and values, then it is not worth risking a better future elsewhere by hanging around. You're not being "crazy" or "too emotional." There is no shame in doing what is best for you. I did.

I was exposed to after-school and community leadership programs as early as elementary school. My mom was a single parent for the first eight years of my life, and it was really important to her as a working mother that I was engaged in activities that would strengthen my confidence and provide me with mentors to encourage my potential. She was also a phenomenal role model for taking risks and relentlessly pursuing developmental opportunities that could open doors and change our lives. One of my earliest memories is of sitting on a stack of telephone books in the copilot seat of a small Cessna airplane while my mom logged miles to earn her private pilot's license. I was about two years old, and it felt as though I was in a real-life adventure movie. Juliette Low, founder of the Girl Scouts of the USA, told girls in 1912 that they could "be anything they wanted to be," including an aviator so it's no surprise between my mother's influence and my experiences as a Girl Scout, I saw no limitations in the pursuit of my goals. At eighteen years old, between my freshman and sophomore years in college, I pursued and earned my pilot's license, which served as more than just an accomplishment but as a testament to my self-esteem, a declaration that I was brave enough to fly toward my goals (literally and figuratively).

My personal values around volunteerism and service, coupled with my mom's influence, continued to be shaped throughout high school and in the bold moves I would later make in my career. These positive influences in my life were most critical during college and the launch of my career as I transitioned from volunteer to board member and from intern to founder, where I had the opportunity to be a role model to young women struggling to find their voice and navigate the tripwires of the corporate world.

The last corporate role I held before launching my business was in the global training and development department. For me, this is where the light bulb turned on, illuminating the possibilities of having greater, scalable impact on the topics that inspired me the most and those I thought most lacking in the workplace. The strength of my external network exposed me to the reality that many women and younger employees were struggling to advance to their potential and that they lacked access to growth and development sponsored by their companies. I was also learning how desperately women need an external confidante to discuss professional issues. We need someone to give us that outsider context and to confide in, someone who can cheer us on and get us fired up—that is what I wanted to be at a larger scale for more women. The energy building up inside me over time through my academic, community, work, and life experiences propelled my decision to run toward a bigger dream: to inspire women and early-career professionals to go after *their* dreams.

When I shared with my direct boss all the efforts I was leading outside the company to support and encourage millennials and women in the workplace, I was told I needed to stop talking about all that stuff and focus on the work in front of me. My boss was basically telling me to stop talking about my career goals, and that's when the timer started ticking— enough was enough—and I had to go after my big idea.

If like me you have a bigger dream you're running toward that requires you to leave your company, go for it! Or if your current experience is robbing you of your ability to do your best work and thrive, and your chances of creating change are nil, by all means, do what you need to do for the sake of your well-being.

If you decide to speak up about harassment or discrimination you are facing in your workplace, I want to emphasize how important it is for you to understand your rights and the processes in your company for handling these issues. This is not my area of expertise, but in my experience, people are not often as knowledgeable about these specifics in their company policies and are discouraged from speaking up by hearsay from colleagues about similar situations that may resemble their own.

Please review your company's employee guidelines to be clear on the process for reporting issues and the protocol for retaliation. You want to be very familiar with your organization's philosophy and values along with the procedures and policies in place to protect you and your well-being as an employee. Know your rights. Know whom you should be speaking to and how things should be handled.

Navigating Your DYHI Decision

This section provides hands on guidance to support your process for making decisions that can change the trajectory of your life and career. It is not to be taken lightly, which is why

I provide you with a diagnostic exercise and a set of reflection questions to urge you to make the time to really prioritize this decision process and think it through to your fullest capacity.

Diagnosing Your Company Culture

When making the decision to dig your heels in (or not), you have to figure out what you're working with. You must diagnose the culture of your company. Culture is made up of the visible and invisible patterns that people follow to communicate, think, and act, which are typically a rear-view mirror reflecting the leadership's preferred behaviors, values, and actions. In many global companies, you may experience a different culture as you move around and interact with different leaders and teams, but there is always a core culture that stems from the central values and mission of the company. Diagnosing your company culture can give you a clear perspective on your company's current and future ability to empower women in an equitable, inclusive environment.

Three Ways to Diagnose Your Company Culture

1. **Dive deeper into behavior.** Reflect on how you and the others involved behaved in situations that made you want to walk out. Think about the people and their vested interests. Is everyone individually coming from a place of authenticity, compassion, and fair intentions?
2. **Explore how people win.** Observe how people gain support and recognition, and think about any potential patterns that are rewarded in your company. Do these appear supportive or damaging for women?

3. **Determine how decisions are made.** Watch closely for when, where, and how decisions are made. Look for trends around where people go to get work done and how meeting times and spaces are used.

The hardest aspects of assessing company culture are understanding how power is distributed (point 2) and how the organization operates (point 3). The hierarchy of decision-making, the career-path structure (rigid or fluid), the distribution of resources (budget, people, and attention), and the company's industry reputation and relevance are factors that can contribute to your diagnosis.

DYHI Reflection Questions

Now that you have taken a deeper dive into your company's culture, you are ready to consider the other important factors in making the decision to dig your heels in. To that end, I have created a DYHI assessment. Disclaimer: This is not an easy checklist that enables me to make the decision for you. There is no ultimate score that makes it obvious what your next step needs to be. That would be in poor judgment on my end, as I don't know all the intimate details of your career and experience at your current employer. But what I have learned is how much we struggle with these decisions in our own head without any guidance and focus on what factors to consider. So the reflection questions shown in the following are intended to support you in gathering all the right data to make your decision, but the choice is ultimately up to you. I want you to own your power in every situation, including this huge decision that will impact on your life, career, and future.

Should I Stay or Should I Go?

* Think about the number of managers you have reported to throughout your tenure.
  * How did the inconsistent or consistent relationship with your managers impact on your acceleration and engagement?
  * How consistent were your reviews, and how has your progress been tracked internally?
  * Do you have an ally in HR or someone who is familiar with talent management at your company who is aware of your career performance, skills, and goals?
* How have you advanced in title and responsibilities?
  * Does the pattern of this advancement line up with your impression of how your career trajectory would unfold when you first joined the organization?
  * How is your advancement similar to or different from that of women and men around you with similar credentials and experience?
* How have you advanced in pay, company equity, and access to additional benefits?
  * When and how often are increases awarded, and were you aware in advance of the timing and details?
  * Did you have any input into these decisions?

* On a daily basis, how do you feel? (If you were to give a 1–5 rating for each of the last five days of work, what would be your average score?)
  * What do you think a reasonable score should be for you to feel engaged and valued? *Note:* The reality is that there will always be challenging days; it's the degree and frequency of these challenges that we must consider in reflecting on our experiences.
* Do you have at least two people you trust and can confide in at work? What were the most memorable conversations you had that had an impact on a decision you made about the possibilities for yourself in your career at your present company?
  * Have you shared challenging situations or moments of self-doubt or frustration with them?
  * Do you know why they choose to stay?
* Do you see business opportunities for your company that leaders are currently not pursuing? How have you stepped up to champion those ideas? Who had your back to support you? Why do you think they did or did not believe in your vision?
  * Do you have access to decision-makers in the areas where you see opportunity?
  * Are there others whom you believe would see your vision as a priority?
* Are you passionate about the industry that surrounds the products and services that your company repre-sents? What is your first memory of a time that illus-trates the connection between your passion and your company's products or services?

- Have you invested time in building connections and relationships external to your company but related to your industry?
- How much influence do those individuals in your external network have in your business?

These questions are intentionally worded to give you time to pause and reflect on the range of factors that weigh on this decision. Thinking holistically about the total work experience and environment will help you determine where you have made progress and where you've experienced barriers. Think about each in terms of the outcomes but also as a test of how much energy you've invested in the areas where you have come up against challenges. Challenge yourself to think of both positive and negative outcomes resulting from the areas these questions explore, such as relationships, growth experiences, engagement, and advancement. Have you engaged all of your allies, the people you trust and those who share your values, in your vision of what the company could be and could do to better serve and support women? Can you rally the energy to push further and demand more in any of the following categories: growth and development, business impact, career advancement, industry involvement?

Wake-Up Calls

Every woman has wake-up-call moments when she decides to make a huge shift in her life, whether it is to dig her heels in and fight for change in her workplace or find a new opportunity that is more deserving of her talents. This section focuses on those critical moments that prompt women to consider walking out. If they do choose to leave, the exercises in the previous chapter are intended to empower them in the decision process so they are not haunted with the regret of lost opportunities for years to come. And if they stay, the stories that follow and throughout the book can fuel their confidence and commitment to their decision.

A wake-up call can strike like lightning; it's experienced quickly, in a fleeting moment in time. After an event or a piece of news, something just clicks in our minds, and suddenly we feel a strong sense of clarity around a decision or situation that may have caused us difficulty or challenged our progress for some time.

Remember Diane, associate dean at Tufts University and former professor at the United States Military Academy? Here's the story of Diane's wake-up call, which she leveraged to dig her heels in while in the army.

Before Diane went to the 82nd Airborne Division in Fort Bragg, North Carolina, for her second assignment she had felt very competent and very confident in her expertise. But now she was faced with a different culture and a different environment, and although her technical skills had some degree of relevance, this job was very different. She told me she affectionately used to call the 82nd division "the he-man women-hater capital of the universe," and her arrival signaled quite a culture shock from her previous assignment in Europe.

This is where special forces and the most elite troops reside. It is one of the most testosterone-laden places in the world. They are highly confident as a result of a very exclusive mission.

Although her assignment ended up being an amazing experience, at first Diane was intimidated and felt out of her depth.

When she showed up on the first day she realized she was one of only two women out of about a hundred people who worked in her building. At that point, women comprised only 2 percent of the entire 82nd. Diane worked in an office called "the fishbowl" because it was in an old, converted officers club where the backside was all glass; her office was next to one of the big floor-to-ceiling windows. Anybody else looking up from the windows across the courtyard could see Diane sitting there prominently in the middle of the organization.

> For my first few years in the army, it didn't occur to me that I was worth less than others simply because of my gender. It wasn't until my second assignment where it became evident that women were getting a raw deal. Your second assignment as an army officer is probably the most important one. It's going to basically determine your career trajectory, where you'll go, and the types of future opportunities open to you. It's the time when officers get selected for company command. You're basically auditioning the entire time.
>
> This is where it became very clear to me that I was going to be perceived as a woman first, and as a soldier second, and that everything I did was representative of my entire gender. I felt this tremendous burden that if I didn't do a good job it would reflect on many more than just me.
>
> I thought it was so important for me to establish myself in knowing all the ins and outs and the minute details of the job that I undervalued the relationships. I failed in establishing those up front and figuring out how I connect with key influencers that would help me make up for the fact that I didn't have a lot of expertise for the particular tasks that I was responsible for.

One day Diane came into work and no one was there. The entire office was a ghost town. She had been really focused on a big project and was working independently, just sending her boss updates from time to time. When she showed up on that fateful day, everyone had departed on a major field exercise for two weeks. She hadn't been included in the planning and wasn't even on the periphery. She had no details at all.

> I just came into work and everybody was gone. Every-
> one. My boss was gone. Our senior non-commissioned
> officer (NCO) was gone. My peer in the office was gone.
> All the other NCOs were gone. I was the stay-back
> person. The phone rang and it was my boss's boss who
> was also my senior rater.

When it is time for the annual performance review, the senior rater's opinion is the only one that matters. Your boss has to be the person who's lobbying for you, advocating for you, and making sure your senior rater knows what your contribution is, Diane told me.

Diane's senior rater told her that there was a big crisis and listed six people in her office he wanted to help with it. He went down to every level stopping just short of the secretary. Diane let him know that everyone was gone to the exercise and she was only person available but ready to help. He paused for a moment then said, "Huh. I guess they took all the heavy hitters, didn't they?"

This was Diane's second interaction with the person who in six months was going to determine her fate and she realized that he did not find her to be a value add.

> I was second class or the JV squad, clearly. That was a
> huge wake-up call to me.

It became very clear to Diane that she needed to engage with her boss when he returned to explain what happened. When she did, he told her she was too focused on her other project and needed to be branching out to establish herself and have a seat at the table. She asked her boss for help with this and to be more involved in other higher-visibility projects. She asked to be kept in the loop of key meetings and to at least be aware of what was going on. Not only did that help her work on those relationships but also it helped her to realize a huge career truth: when you're going through transitions, you need to focus on who can help you fill in the gaps as opposed to just putting your head down and trying to learn everything yourself.

Leveraging Your Wake-Up Call

Wake-up calls or epiphanies—and whether and how we learn from them—have been studied by psychologists at Ohio State University. They created a game and then monitored external behaviors such as pupil dilation as their subjects started to play against their opponents. Some of the players based their strategy on reading their opponents and guessing their next moves; others based theirs on reacting quickly to new information that appeared on their computer screens during the game. The psychologists found that the players who were focused on reading their opponents showed little physiological change during the game; by contrast, the players who reacted to information change had significant pupil dilation (which indicated epiphany moments) as the information registered on their screens and triggered their next action; the dilation disappeared after they had committed to their next move. Ian Krajbich, a coauthor of the study and assistant professor of psychology and economics, concluded that it is better to think carefully about how to solve a problem than to spend time paying attention to what opponents or competitors are doing.[1]

Here's my takeaway: We derive value from an epiphany or wake-up call by looking within. We can use our wake-up calls to make the right decisions for our lives if we are aware of our true feelings and instincts around the situations in which they arise.

Three Steps to Leveraging Epiphany Learning as a Compass for Your Career

Step 1: Avoid any knee-jerk decisions and slow down to allow yourself the time to evaluate the situation. (Me to you: "Did that just happen?!")

Step 2: Acknowledge that the wake-up call or epiphany struck a nerve and therefore deserves your attention and is not something to sweep aside (Me to you: "You are not crazy.")

Step 3: Reflect on the factors surrounding the wake-up call or epiphany to determine your best next move. (Me to you: "You've got this; your next move matters most.")

My Wake-Up Call

After a series of disappointing exchanges with one of my senior leaders back in the days of my corporate career, I was ready to walk right out the door forever . . . but instead I hit the pause button. I took a step back to acknowledge that something wasn't right for me and that this was a feeling that I could no longer ignore. I took inventory of several occasions when I had felt the same pit in my stomach and heaviness on my heart. But I also wanted to make a smart decision, as it would have a huge impact on my career and life. I couldn't quite pinpoint whether it was the culture, the leadership, or the systems that frustrated me most when I thought about my future in that organization. By allowing myself some time to evaluate and reflect on the situation, I realized that I had experienced the compounding impact of several different occasions leading up to this most recent wake-up call.

Two months earlier, I had been asked to develop and facilitate a two-day training program on cystic fibrosis, a disease state that had actually killed two members of my family before they both turned thirty-five years old. Had I been tapped intentionally as an opportunity to invite my personal experiences into the learnings and help the company leverage my insights to better serve patients and our colleagues who would be working on a drug to treat it? Nope, it was purely a coincidence; but, nonetheless, I still approached senior leaders suggesting that, during the training sessions, we open up the dialogue to include the journey of families who had also encountered this disease and share its impact. Regrettably, I was told to stick to the "science" and not involve my experience. This was all about "execution, not inspiration."

Have you ever felt a really strong disconnect between your personal experiences and how it was leveraged to influence the work or services of your company? I certainly felt that because of my own family's struggles and lack of resources and knowledge, I could add much more to our efforts to be what our patients and their families needed.

There was also the time I had been made to feel guilty for not wanting to attend a leadership meeting scheduled to take place in Florida the week prior to a critical product launch in New York. This launch was an enormous undertaking and the highest priority, yet I convinced myself that this all-male team must really value my perspective to make such a big deal about my attendance. I can still hear my internal little-girl voice:

"They need me!" So I booked my flight and headed south, full of ideas and the data to support them, only to realize within the first half hour what my true role was meant to be.

Phew, Joan made it. Can you flip-chart and record the takeaways from the sessions?

Literally, and with straight faces, this had been their expectation for me, despite the fact that I was the third most senior person in the room. My boss actually followed me out and indirectly apologized for the situation while offering to discuss my career interests upon our return to New York.

I let that dangling carrot distract me from my frustration at the time and was only reminded of it during a conversation with Neela Montgomery, CEO of Crate and Barrel, whom I recently interviewed for ForbesWomen. Neela shared the moment when she made the decision to dig her heels in.

When I was twenty-seven years old, I presented at my first board of directors meeting for my organization. I was extremely prepared and optimistic, but the experience was horrible. They weren't constructive, to say it mildly. And I literally walked out of the room full of men and said, "I am done. I will never be spoken to like that again. I don't aspire to be like anyone in that room."

The CEO came out of the room and apologized. He said to me, "If you just stay angry or leave in frustration, it won't make the difference. Your job is to change this and one day be in that room. You can choose to stay and fight for change from the inside."

No judgment either way, but I was motivated to ensure that none of the women to follow me would ever feel the way I had and be treated in that manner. Ten years later, I became a board member and full circle prioritized my mission to ensure the experience for women at that company was incredibly different.

With her eyes wide open to the critical need to be an advocate for equality and inclusion at the most senior levels,

Neela continues to be a trailblazing leader for women in her organization and industry.

> Think about the worst thing to happen when you take a risk: You might fail, and you might fail visibly. It's easier to take a risk when you realize that what you do is not who you are. The more successful you are, the more risk you have. It's important to encourage each other when you think you're playing it safe and lean into your network to push you. A former boss said to me that leadership is what other people need from you, not what you need from them. That's the difference between management and leadership: use your energy to give to others what they need, as it's the only way you can succeed as a leader.

At my crossroad, I also reflected on a story that was not just my own but had impacted on me equally as much. Britt was a highly gifted communicator, invaluable team player, and all-around high-potential creative contributor on my team. Despite two bouts with cancer, she had completed her MBA at night (unsponsored by our employer) and was way overdue for a title promotion. Britt and I had met on a number of occasions to discuss the impact of her work so that I could write a six-page document detailing examples of her stellar performance. As I reflected on the email trails and on the numerous meetings I had hustled to schedule with anyone who could remotely influence or control the process, I realized that this grueling effort had panned out. Finally. After eight months. Britt had patiently waited for an update, all the while continuing to execute all of her goals and work her responsibilities beyond expectations. The topper for me was that even though she had been granted a promotion in title, the company had decided it didn't justify any bump in her pay. Britt had been pleased to finally have her title match her talent, but it hadn't been enough for me. I knew that she deserved more, but I felt helpless without any control or capacity to give it to her.

This was the epiphany moment that inspired Britt and me to launch a Lean In Circle, a small group of women who meet monthly to share their ambitions and support each other.[2] We invited women at our peer level and those at earlier career stages across diverse industries. At the time, I was seven months pregnant with my first daughter. The preparation in advance and experience of coming together monthly were encouraging, enlightening, and even emotional. We covered such topics as negotiation, work-life balance, managing gender bias, and leadership. I'll never forget the first meeting held a couple months after my daughter was born and the stories we all chose to share beyond motherhood but related to life transitions that impact on careers. Being a part of a tribe of women supported by the incredible resources from the Lean In organization gave me career confidence and enhanced my clarity about the big bold changes I wanted to lead for more women.

Clearing Some Headspace for Positive Self-Talk

I know the world has told you that your flighty and emotional reactions make you a risky bet when it comes to promotion, advancement, and increased authority. Yet there is no significant evidence to imply that women make their decisions based on some inexplicable feeling or inner hunch. In thirty-two studies that looked at how men and women thought through a problem or decision, twelve of the studies found that women were more analytical than men.[3] Clearly we can be confident about our ability to use our natural judgment and critical thinking skills. This research found that women systematically turned to the data, whereas men were more inclined to go with their gut, hunches, or intuitive reactions. The other twenty studies found no difference between men and women's thinking styles.[4]

A marked strength that women bring to decision-making is their analytical perseverance and shrewdness, which may often start with a wake-up call and be followed up with careful research. This knowledge should give you some breathing room to understand that you are just as data driven and analytical as a man, if not more so. I hope that this awareness gives you confidence in your ability to control the outcome you want.

Don't dismiss your own voice when you have a wake-up call. If you find yourself in one of those moments when you feel as though you've reached your limit, trust your ability to decide what is truly best for you. Embrace the lesson rising within you and know that it is important, albeit uncomfortable, right now.

Part 2
MAKING IT HAPPEN

The best way to predict the future . . . is to create it.

—Peter Drucker

Setting the Stage for Success

In this chapter you will
* **Visualize your career goals**
* **Clarify what you need from your day-to-day experiences**
* **Envision your role and influence in a new environment that works for you**

Digging your heels in works best if you begin with a clear vision and intention in mind. You must first imagine the possibilities you see for yourself in order to visualize what your company will look like when this transformation occurs. There is substantial scientific evidence to support the use of visualization in improving performance and attaining goals. Many successful people, from athletes such as US soccer player Mia Hamm, who retired with a world-record 158 international goals, to twenty-five-time Emmy Award winner Oprah Winfrey, have found that brain imagery informs their real-life actions and inspires personal follow-through.

> **If you don't know where you are going, then you will not know what actions to take.**
>
> —*Mia Hamm*

Amanda Apodaca, business transformation advisor for Lilly USA, admitted to me that getting clear on what she wants has been the most challenging and the most rewarding factor in her career.

> Every single pivotal point in my career is when I got extremely clear on what I wanted and when I mustered up the courage to ask for it.

She recalled her first job out of college at a TV station, when she was having lunch with her peers and they began talking about the promotions they were being considered for. She was taken aback because the promotion conversation had never come up for her. When she finally asked her boss why they hadn't discussed promotions, he told her, "I never knew it was something you wanted."

> Interestingly enough, I got the promotion, but what if I would've had more clarity on what my next step was sooner, and I had asked for it sooner? There's this theme for me, as I look back over my career, of sitting in the box, not ruffling everybody's feathers, trying to work hard. And I just wish I would've known the level of ownership that I could take over my career.

Take a cue from Mia and Amanda and begin to visualize where you want to go in your career. It may be helpful to think about people inside and outside your company who inspire you.

* Who has a career that you find appealing?
* Which aspects of their success do you want to replicate in your own life and career?
* What has been their impact on their company, their industry, or the world at large?

As you contemplate these questions, I will share the stories of two women who were able to achieve their visions.

Building Your Dream Title

Theresa Batiller has worked for a global healthcare company for fifteen years. She was hired straight from receiving her undergraduate degree at Rutgers School of Engineering. Theresa always aspired to work for her company and saw herself employed there for her entire career. But there was a moment when she considered looking outside the big corporation.

> Ever since I was in college, I thought I wanted to be a lifer at this company. I applied only here. I wanted to retire here. So, for me to think about leaving, that was a big deal.

Early in Theresa's career in the supply chain division of of this global healthcare company, she was told that in order to advance in her field, she must spend significant time working at a manufacturing site, learning the day-to-day operations of manufacturing facilities and navigating issues as a plant manager. However, all of the manufacturing sites were in locations that posed a challenge for Theresa: Puerto Rico, Mexico, and Europe.

Why were they a challenge? First, Theresa has a very successful working spouse, who would have to give up his job if they relocated. Second, she has a young daughter with special needs who is confined to a wheelchair and requires specific medical monitoring and therapy. Theresa couldn't pick up and move just anywhere, because her family needs communities and resources that are handicap accessible. In New Jersey, where they have lived for the duration of her career thus far, they have immediate family nearby who help with her daughter and younger son.

> My limitations were that I had to be near a major airport because my husband travels a lot. I wanted to be in the United States because I am most comfortable with the handicap resources and rules here. Even though I was open to relocating, those two criteria alone precluded me from relocating to a manufacturing site. I was getting really discouraged, as I am very career ambitious.

Because Theresa felt she couldn't move into a direct man-ufacturing role, she took on positions and responsibilities in functions such as planning, project management, and qual-ity engineering where she could get indirect exposure to the process. She also took on leadership roles outside her day-job responsibilities to increase her exposure and visibility, such as leading the employee resource group for young profes-sionals. She even led the first-ever internal hackathon at her company. That variety of experiences helped her gain an "end-to-end" view.

Finally, Theresa was given advice that struck gold. A female senior leader and mentor stated something that transformed how Theresa thought about her career.

> She asked me, "Well what do you want to do?" That was part of my problem. I didn't know exactly what I wanted to do. I know I wanted to move up, to make a big impact somewhere in supply chain. I didn't know exactly what specific function it would be.

The thing that changed my mind was this advice. It was, "You don't need to change for this company."

Theresa felt empowered, and stopped seeing her needs as limitations. She began considering what her company needed to be for her to continue advancing to her potential. She visualized the actions she needed to take to secure a role that would give her more manufacturing oversight—on her terms. And she approached her bosses with the conviction to make it happen.

Theresa's first step was to seek out people who had gained exposure in manufacturing without taking on-site roles. She was pleasantly surprised by the diversity in their experiences. In about four months, Teresa was presented a role with requirements that she typically would have been hesitant to pursue. The job qualifications and previous incumbent leaders followed a very traditional profile; these leaders had "grown up" on manufacturing sites and were certified Six Sigma Black Belts (a highly prized process improvement certification). Theresa neither fit the traditional profile nor had any of those experiences. But she had a pretty compelling vision for the department and how she could lead a transformation.

The title of the role was director of process excellence. Process excellence is all about improving the manufacturing sites—for example, by looking for areas of waste and ways to increase efficiency. Theresa had been exposed to various initiatives focused on culture change, and she had unique skills and a passion for this work. As she looked at her company, an enormous global organization, she knew it faced the traditional hierarchical challenges that slow down change initiatives—and she knew she could make a difference.

> This job was perfect for what I needed. I could be remote. It would get me closer to manufacturing. All my teams are in manufacturing facilities. I still get that option of flying to the manufacturing sites, but I don't have to be full-time in one.

As the new director, Theresa was given the opportunity to transform the group. Using her creative vision of her department's role in helping her company become more agile, one of the first things she did was rebrand from process excellence to business excellence. The group is now focused on how they impact on the business overall—on finding inefficiencies not just in the manufacturing processes but across all business processes.

Takeaways from Theresa's Story

* **Be bold and speak up.** Theresa expressed her needs and articulated them clearly to senior leadership. She needed her company to provide more flexibility within key roles in order for her to deliver results while maintaining her family priorities.

* **Think values, not limitations.** Theresa shifted from viewing herself as having limitations to having clear values, which sharpened her previously blurry vision for her future. Like Theresa, strive for a vision of how high you want to advance your career, a vision that works in harmony with your values. Then you can chart the skills you want to hone, the relationships you want to build, and the changes that need to be made in your organization for you to get there.

* **Be clear on your unique career vision.** Theresa had a clear vision for moving up the corporate ladder, and she knew that it required her to obtain manufacturing experience.

She also knew she couldn't relocate to a manufacturing site. So she found a way to gain that experience without relocating. Clarity around her vision for what she desired and what she deserved was what ultimately helped Theresa secure the role she needed in order to dig her heels in at her company.

Theresa has been approached multiple times by less tenured women who confide in her about their perceived limitations. She empowers them to think beyond the traditional career road map.

> I used to overmanage my career. I'd be thinking to myself that I'm going to go for this job, then here, then over there! It never turned out like I wanted it to. It would be so frustrating because I never got the job I wanted in my order and timeline.
>
> It's actually interesting, because now the advice I'm giving other people is completely opposite to what I was being given early in my career. I no longer view my situation, or other women in similar situations, as a limitation. It has been a huge awakening for me.

Identifying the Gaps and Filling Them

Stephanie Epstein is the chief operating officer (COO) for the global marketing organization at BlackRock, the world's largest asset management firm. She has spent almost sixteen years at the firm and transitioned into her current role in 2017.

Stephanie is one of the most influential and accomplished millennial women in the financial services industry. She is someone who seizes opportunities even when there is no clear pathway or guarantee of success. The pathway to securing her former role as chief of staff for BlackRock's president Rob Kapito was a catalyst for her leadership, as it gave her a global platform to test her ideas and build her reputation for evolving the culture at BlackRock. She credits the opportunity to become a chief of staff and design the impact of the role as being afforded the freedom to craft her vision.

In 2010, Charlie Hallac, copresident of BlackRock and the architect of its industry-leading investment operating system, Aladdin, gave Stephanie a blank piece of paper. Literally. As a vice president in the acquisitions group, Stephanie had worked with Charlie over a five-year period during the company's efforts to integrate several acquisitions, including State Street Research, Merrill Lynch, and Barclays, with the goal of ensuring that the client experience remained a consistent priority and focus. Charlie and Rob needed someone with client experience to help them with their day-to-day responsibilities in running and operating the firm, and they let Stephanie be the one to build out the role. The vision she wrote out on that piece of paper was the basic framework for a strategy of how a chief of staff function would increase efficiency and effectiveness across the entire organization.

This experience represented a consistent theme across Stephanie's career: identifying a gap she was confident she could fill while cultivating sponsor relationships to further enable and empower her along the way. Her story brings clarity to the idea of sponsorship, which is an elusive concept for many women looking to access relationships with influential leaders. As sponsors, Charlie and Rob provided the air cover and a launch pad for Stephanie's talents, but it was without a doubt her talents and creativity that catapulted her career.

Finding ways to provide value without being asked to be is my first piece of advice. Because if I was just going to

sit back and wait to be told to do X, Y, and A, I wouldn't have gotten anywhere. These leaders (Rob and Charlie) are very busy, and they've got a lot of things to do. So I was trying to find ways or find those gaps within their office that I could fill and make their jobs easier.

I was constantly trying to figure out throughout the organization who were going to be my partners to help develop and deliver our vision. I was listening to Rob, listening to Charlie, and going on a massive tour to figure out who my allies and partners would be to help me build the infrastructure. And then I started to build an actual operation and design resources like briefing templates and talking-point frameworks for key client meetings, which are now standard aspects of running the business today. At the time, we didn't have anything like that. Once you see your ideas actually working and coming to life with a positive correlated impact, then it gives you the confidence to take on more.

Stephanie's vision also required rolling out a number of key culture-related initiatives. First, she developed a program called the VP Village in the Americas. With a runway to experiment and design, she hosted a series of dinners to explore what employees needed.

It was the summer of 2011, and I had BBQs every single Monday night. I would host VPs in a conference room, and just listen hard to what they wanted more of from BlackRock's culture.

Through these conversations, a vision emerged to help VPs build their own network, a village to strengthen their connections to one another. Stephanie got VP Village up and running, and scaled it globally; it still exists today as one of the strongest employee networks at BlackRock. Next, she led the design of an onboarding program for managing directors (MDs). Once again, there was a gap she saw in transitioning MDs and finding an optimal approach of experiences and trainings to set them up for success. This onboarding program, created in

2012, still exists today helping MDs build their network beyond the silo of their sole function. Finally, Stephanie led the
creation of a rewards and recognition program that is currently in its fifth year. It celebrates employees who exhibit the
BlackRock principles, including a special award called the
Heart of BlackRock; winners are given the opportunity to
hold personal mentoring sessions with Rob Kapito.

The long-term viability of her ideas is a marker of
Stephanie's career. And the programs she has created have a
consistent theme linked to her own journey, which is to help
people make stronger and broader connections. Stephanie
herself is a connector, and her energy is fueled by pioneering
new ideas that result from bringing together diverse perspectives. Her efforts have encouraged the creation of diverse close-
knit teams, which are a cornerstone of BlackRock's culture.

No one told Stephanie that these efforts were part of her
job description or even that any of them were in her scope,
but she had that blank sheet of paper that boosted her confidence and gave her the courage to pursue the programs
that she felt were aligned with the firm's values and goals.
The opportunity to explore from the expansive viewpoint
of the office of the president was a privilege she did not take
for granted.

Takeaways from Stephanie's Story

* **Find the gaps only you can fill.** Stephanie learned to
  match her unique strengths to the gaps she identified in her
  company's business model. You may not always find leaders who will give you that blank piece of paper, so do it for
  yourself up front. Map out your strengths. Think about your
  company and if there are any clear gaps such as those that

limit efficiency, innovation, or collaboration. Initiate a dialogue with your boss and senior leaders to show them the results that only you can drive with your strengths to fill those gaps.

* **Take initiative in the process.** Stephanie observed, "I've never been in a job here where it's been like, 'Here are the five things you're supposed to do.' Like never! To some people, this would freak them out. But it's never been the case. And even in my current job, no one gave me my task list of ten things that define what a COO does. I have to add my own flavor to anything I pursue. And you always have to. Here at BlackRock, the culture really supports this."

* **Seek feedback along the way.** Proactively asking for feedback then navigating what you receive are critical actions for women looking to advance. Stephanie sought out feedback every ninety days, asking, "Is this working? What isn't working?" Tweaking was necessary, and others' giving feedback also heightened their investment in the process as she in turn used that input to make improvements. (For more on feedback as an opportunity to grow, read chapter 6.)

Creating Your Future in Seven Steps

Now that you have a clearer vision of your career goals at your company, let's begin exploring how to realize that vision. The following steps are the foundation you need to dig your heels in. You must first know where you are, where you want to go, the resources you have to get there, and the resources you need to obtain.

Step 1: Take a Personal Inventory

> **Any kind of personal transformation that ultimately results in you becoming a more resonant leader—and sustaining it—begins with some kind of a challenge to your mindfulness, a growing awareness of your passion, beliefs, duties, and your true calling.**
>
> —*Annie McKee*, Resonant Leadership

Define the three attributes you value in yourself that translate into strengths at work. Pick qualities that allow you to stay true to your most authentic self. Then describe how those attributes make you feel and what they look like in action. Here are mine:

1. Credibility and experience. These help me at work to suggest best practices based on the case studies where I saw successes or failures. I can use data points from my client and work experiences to help others understand my perspective and to back up the ideas I present to help them in similar situations.

2. Being an encouraging and positive but direct mentor. I know how important it is to have people in your corner who give you energy and who may see more for you than you imagined was possible for yourself. I'm energized by empowering others and helping them dream bigger by telling them what I see for their potential and future. My unique style can be quite direct. This stems from my own preference for direct feedback; I don't do well with those who are vague or who beat around the bush. If I want you to

succeed, I want to help you be aware of your blind spots, and I'm committed to being an honest coach in developing the skills you need to break through.

3. Being super-focused. This may be akin to my Virgo type A personality, but I am someone who follows through. I don't drop the ball, I multitask, and I shoot for the stars. It's hard to find my off switch at times (except when it comes to being present for my kids), but this sets me up to be a reliable partner and strong ally at work on urgent deadlines and large-scale projects.

Step 2: Map Your Goals

Someone recently interviewed me and asked me to think about my best days at work, then share the consistent factors in those memories that I could replicate when working to meet future goals. It became clear to me that I am energized by

* New experiences that expose me to new places and groups of people I am unfamiliar with (new industry, new job pathway, new culture, and so on)
* Opportunities to share my ideas at scale with the potential to reach diverse audiences
* A high level of interaction with people who are open to inspiration and experiences that give them the courage to make bolder moves and find their voice
* People around me who laugh a lot and share honest advice about how they juggle the demands of work and life
* Seeing a clear connection between my work and its impact on girls and younger women

Taking time to imagine feeling and experiencing these important elements more often and picturing how I could pursue them made it crystal clear to me that they are critical to my success and happiness. This meant that I had to continue to ensure they were present in the work I pursued and how I spent my time.

Now it's your turn. Visualize a good but challenging day in your current role. What is energizing for you in this scenario that you can replicate in your efforts to meet future goals?

Step 3: Reimagine Your Company

Imagine your company operating in a way that allows you to thrive. Visualize the transformation within your company, your department, your boss, and your colleagues. Picture the collective state of your company post-transformation as being more inclusive, inspiring, and equitable. Describe it in four different ways that create an emotional connection:

* How it aligns with your personal mission
* What makes it the company you deserve
* How it is leading change across your industry
* How it makes a broader impact in the communities it serves

Eva Tansky Blum is someone I have admired and been lucky to call a mentor for almost twenty-five years. She was president of the University of Pittsburgh Alumni Association during my time as a student. Eva held numerous executive-level leadership positions during her thirty-seven-year career at PNC Bank and last served as the executive vice president and director of community affairs before retiring. In 2015, Eva was elected chair of the University of Pittsburgh Board of Trustees and is the first woman in the university's history to hold this position. With all of those professional accomplishments, you can see why she was someone who inspired my career, but it was her ability to connect her company to the community that drove her most significant accomplishment that is most dear to my heart.

Eva served as the president of the PNC Foundation and championed the vision for PNC's Grow Up Great, a $350 million, fourteen-plus-year program that supports quality childhood education. Working with Sesame Street Workshop and The Fred Rogers Company, Grow Up Great created "Learning is Everywhere," a free, comprehensive, bilingual program designed to help prepare children—particularly underserved children—for success in school and life. The Grow Up Great journey has been extraordinary for PNC as it helped to shape the corporate culture and provided a platform to engage PNC leadership and employees locally. Most important, over four million disadvantaged children are learning more and being exposed to exciting, new things such as ballet, opera, art, performing arts, and science. In their partnership with The Fred Rogers Company Eva and the PNC team helped with training employee volunteers. Since Grow Up Great's 2004 inception, more than 61,000 PNC employees have volunteered, and approximately 747,000 volunteer hours have been logged at early childhood education centers. This can be credited to the progressive policy at PNC that permits up to forty hours of paid time off for volunteerism. Research[1] shows that in children's early years, opportunities to interact with caring, responsive adults are of utmost importance. Eva's mission to help the PNC Foundation have an enduring impact in a very focused area cultivated PNC's imperative that all children have the opportunity to enter kindergarten ready to learn and enhanced the urgency to provide access to quality early education. She believed that an investment in the workforce of tomorrow makes economic sense today.

Step 4: Identify Resources

What internal, company, and industry resources can you leverage to help create change and move your organization forward? Here are some examples:

* Company women's network or employee resource groups
* Local professional women's organizations
* Collaborative and inclusive colleagues
* Company culture initiatives, change management programs, or training efforts to evolve your company's culture or increase awareness around diversity and inclusion

If you have not spent any time looking into these resources, attending their events, or pursuing a leadership role, then give yourself a deadline of thirty days to make the move to learn more and get involved.

Step 5: Invest in Content and Connections

Empower your efforts and support your goals by strengthening your knowledge and relationships around organizational change. (See "Events and Organizations to Explore" for a list of conferences targeted at professional working women.)

Events and Organizations to Explore

* Alt Summit
* Black Women of Enterprise Power Network
* C2: ColorComm
* Create + Cultivate
* Diversity Inc.
* Ellevate Network
* EmpowerHer for Black Women
* Forbes Women's Summit
* Fortune: The Most Powerful Women & Most Powerful Women Next Gen
* GirlBoss Rally
* Grace Hopper Celebration of Women in Computing
* Healthcare Businesswomen's Association (HBA)
* ICAN's annual Women's Leadership Conference
* The Influence Network
* Makers
* Massachusetts Conference for Women
* National Coalition of 100 Black Women, Inc.
* National Congress of Black Women
* Pennsylvania Conference for Women
* Powerful Women's Weekend
* Propel Women
* S.H.E. Summit
* SXSW
* TED Women
* Texas Conference for Women
* WIN Summit
* Women in the World
* Women of Color Leadership and Empowerment Conference (WOC)
* Yellow Conference

Every year, I pick two conferences that I have not attended before, and, if they're affordable, I try to attend in person or virtually (many conferences offer a cheaper digital ticket) or reach out to someone on a panel to learn more afterward. It's really not that hard to look up the names of the people speaking at an event and find their contact information and get in touch. The hard part is mustering up the nerve to make a move to speak to people we don't know. Use LinkedIn. Find their profiles and send a link to connect, but be sure to include a personal message. And if you're nervous about making the first move, what's the worst that could happen? They don't respond? Not a big deal in the long run.

Step 6: Seek Out Other Women to Learn about Their Vision

Find your tribe. Connect with other women and learn how their visions for their careers may align with yours. This step is absolutely critical. You need groups of women (and men) in all roles at your company to care about the case for change.

Have you ever noticed when you attend conferences that most key business meetings have a theme—"Go Beyond," "Excel Together," and the like—that they use across the entire event and in all their marketing materials? They brand it like crazy leading up to the meeting and throughout the entire experience to align everyone to a common goal. Doing so creates a language for the success they want to achieve. Try this as a motivation technique for yourself and use it to connect with others. Identify a mantra or a quote that resonates with your own journey. I'm not suggesting you wear it like a sign on meeting new connections but use it more as a personal reminder of what really matters to you. It may come up organically in a coffee conversation or when you are meeting with a group of women for a project. I've often been inspired by a leader or a colleague who drove home her point with a memorable quote.

> **I've learned that people will forget what you said, people will forget what you did, but people will never forget how you made them feel.**
>
> —*Maya Angelou*

Step 7: Make the Case for Your Company

Think through what your company currently looks like, what it needs to look like to support your vision, and what it will take for the company to transform.

* What are the gender stats in your company?
* How do they compare to those of other companies?
* What are the benefits of increasing the number of women in senior leadership roles across every department?

Collect the data to support your vision for yourself and for your company! Refer to The Business Case for Change data points located in the back of the book.

Here is advice from Michelle Carnahan of Sanofi on how to shine a light on gender inequity in your company.

Five Ways You Can Champion the Gender Lens in Your Business

1. **Take the emotion out of it and bring the facts into it.** Many times when you think about being gender smart in your company, it really does boil down to, "We're working on a business, and it is a dollars-and-cents solution we're talking about." The data and the dollars and cents are friendly to the need for a gender-balanced workforce.

2. **Get some victories behind you.** There are going to be times when you advocate and go out on a limb for a female mentee or employee, and these women succeed at fixing a big issue in the business. Make those victories public. Get those victories to back up the message so that there is no doubt that what you're doing is good for the business, not just good in a self-serving way. Never lose the focus that diversity and inclusion are about the greater good for the company.

3. **Hold women accountable for lifting other women up.** When you see women shying away from standing up for someone just because she is a woman and they don't want to be perceived as too much of a feminist, call them out—not in a nasty, public way; it doesn't have to be a negative confrontation, but it has to be a real confrontation: "Why?" and "How can I help you?" You need to help them understand how having them on board will create change across the organization that benefits everybody. And, of course, you need to be the cheerleader applauding other women's efforts to lift as they climb.

4. Don't be afraid to say the hard things. The hardest thing can be to point out when what's happening today is not okay. For example, one of the hard things I've said over the course of my career, which a lot of people still don't like, is that I don't love it when professional men say, "I want to help women because I think about my daughter." This may be seen by some as a positive or innocent thing, to think of someone else taking responsibility for our well-being. But I'm a woman in her late forties. I don't know that my greatest comparator is someone's eighteen-year-old daughter. I never hear a man say to my male colleagues in their late forties, "When I think of your situation, I think of my son." Many workplace cultures are still based in paternalism, which is defined as "'the practice of controlling employees or citizens in a way that is similar to that of a father controlling his children, by giving them what is beneficial but not allowing them responsibility or freedom of choice.'" Framing is important in helping ensure that women are viewed as autonomous, fully capable professionals, not merely seen in terms of their relationship to a man, as paternalism does.

5. Keep pushing for change. Always.

Keeping Space for You in the Process

On your path to creating your future, be vulnerable with your vision and compassionate toward yourself. I wasn't, and it held me back from appreciating my hard-fought journey.

If you looked at my resume, you would see a solid story of success. I was selected into international leadership programs and won national writing competitions in high school. I was elected student government president at a huge university. I had multiple job offers before graduation, where I was the student speaker in front of all my friends and their families. And, as I shared earlier, I even earned my pilot's license at eighteen years old! Through hard work and perseverance, I was promoted six times in my thirteen-year corporate career.

But during that career climb, I never saw those successes clearly. There was no playbook to prep me for the real challenges I would face in the workplace and in figuring out how to juggle them with my personal life. I let every setback overshadow every success in my mind. With each milestone, I was flooded shortly after with a feeling of disappointment that this next thing didn't fully satisfy me. I kept second-guessing my decisions, my goals, and my path. When I was in sales, I wanted to be in marketing. When I was in marketing, I wanted to be in training. And when I was in training, I wanted to spend more time designing programs. This pattern of "never enough" was suffocating and distracting at times.

I remember many moments in my twenties and early thirties when I would be discouraged or hard on myself, feeling as though I would never achieve my ultimate goals. Deeply disappointed in the rocky road to progressing toward the next career level, I felt as if I had to change who I was just to advance. This made me fearful of sharing my biggest dreams with other people, particularly when I decided to step out on my own with Why Millennials Matter. I succumbed both to the fear of being vulnerable about what I really wanted out of life and to the super-sized pressure I put on myself to be perfect.

Look in the mirror and decide if you are in that place right now. If so, please remember that big bold moves and authenticity matter, as you will see in the next chapter, but even small steps forward in full alignment to your values and true motivators will help you get to the place you deserve.

> **I stumble and fall, and I constantly find myself needing to change course. And even though I'm trying to follow a map that I've drawn, there are many times when frustration and self-doubt take over, and I wad up that map and shove it into the junk drawer in my kitchen. It's not an easy journey from excruciating to exquisite, but for me it's been worth every step.**
>
> —*Brené Brown,* Daring Greatly

Big Bold Moves

In this chapter, you will learn
* **What to do and how to begin creating the big bold change you deserve in your organization**

We all want to work somewhere that treats people fairly and where we feel that our voice matters equally without our being dismissed because of our age, gender, or race. But where and how do you actually start chipping away at companies that have been operating in a different mode for decades or more? How can you take the first steps to disrupt the current culture dynamics and help your organization pivot to become a more inclusive, equitable environment? Where do you start? How do you find the time to be a catalyst for all of this and still do your day job?

The Playbook

Here is your playbook for pulling together the key insights into how you can design the career you desire and, through your actions, transform your company to be the one you deserve. Keep each of the following eight big bold moves in mind as you go through your days, identifying which action is appropriate to take when, within the context of your life and professional situation.

* Model inclusive leadership
* Take control of your growth and development
* Engage your women's network
* Lift as you climb
* Ignite an industry-wide conversation
* Accelerate toward equal representation
* Get pay straight
* Advocate behind closed doors

Model Inclusive Leadership

Have you ever heard the phrase, "Start local, grow global"? The same goes for corporate culture and the employee behaviors that reinforce what is valued and what is not. Let's "start local" by taking a hard look at your relationship behaviors at work and those of the teams you are a part of, whether as a leader or an individual contributor. The most influential strategy to improve inclusion across your team is to model how certain behaviors deliver better results for everyone. Someone has to connect the dots; this is your opportunity. Your commitment to seeing this through will test you at times, but it will be worth the effort to improve your environment day by day.

If you can help your team evolve to a place where everyone feels included and engaged and is performing at the top of her or his game, then you become a center for excellence and an influential North Star for others. That all starts with your commitment to be at your best and leverage strengths that are both inclusive of those around you and true to what energizes you.

Use the diagram here to guide your exploration of how you interact with your team and how your interactions impact on your own engagement and performance. Devote time to thinking about the situations you encounter, the people you meet, and the feedback you receive. Think about a one-on-one you had last week with a team member, a conversation with a colleague, or a recent team meeting where your own boss was present. Force yourself to think about how others impact on you, and how you impact on them. Take notes somewhere private so that you can cite specific individuals, attributes, and feelings to clearly identify key situations and behaviors that lift you up versus those that may let you down.

The goal here is to gain an understanding of how you experience those with whom you interact most often. This is why the figure encourages you to reflect on interactions with the various people whom you see at work the most. You could even add clients or suppliers to the mix as well to really evaluate how daily interactions fuel or deplete your energy. As you begin to discover areas where you experience challenges and feel the most in conflict with being your authentic self, you can develop a plan to strengthen your own presence. You may not be able to change other people overnight but you can send a clear message about authenticity and inclusion when you are

Inclusive Leadership Model

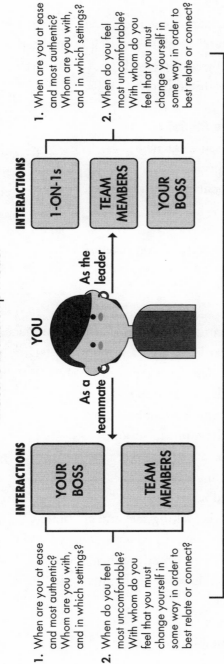

YOU

As a teammate ← → *As the leader*

INTERACTIONS

| YOUR BOSS |
| TEAM MEMBERS |

1. When are you at ease and most authentic? Whom are you with, and in which settings?

2. When do you feel most uncomfortable? With whom do you feel that you must change yourself in some way in order to best relate or connect?

INTERACTIONS

| 1-ON-1s |
| TEAM MEMBERS |
| YOUR BOSS |

1. When are you at ease and most authentic? Whom are you with, and in which settings?

2. When do you feel most uncomfortable? With whom do you feel that you must change yourself in some way in order to best relate or connect?

3. How do the interactions that give you positive energy impact your day-to-day experience and ultimately your performance?

4. How do the interactions that deplete your energy and stifle your authenticity impact your day-to-day experience and ultimately your performance?

5. Have you ever thought about how you influence others in these same settings? Would they report the same feelings that you do?

able to role-model your values for appreciating diverse perspectives and people. You will be able to get clear on where and how you can best lead by example with positive, inclusive behaviors such as the ones listed here.[1]

Inclusive Behaviors to Model

* Demonstrates high self-awareness
* Exhibits high humility
* Demonstrates an openness to difference
* Shares power
* Is accessible
* Exhibits strong cross-cultural competence
* Displays courage
* Is cooperative
* Is flexible
* Leads constructive conflict (ensures that task conflicts are resolved in ways that leave all team members feeling respected and heard) *Note:* This tends to be the most challenging trait for leaders to embody.
* Empowers team members to make decisions
* Takes advice from those on the ground
* Deploys empathy to ensure that everyone gets heard
* Shares credit for team success
* Gives actionable feedback
* Builds trust, makes risk-taking safe and celebrated
* Displays interpersonal integrity (makes decisions and interacts with people in a consistent manner; solicits feedback and honest discussion despite its being inconvenient or uncomfortable for self)
* Supports team growth
* Fosters team accountability

How to Start Modeling Inclusive Leadership[2]

* Focus on people you work with who have responsibilities and tasks that are largely independent
* Check in on them to better understand how connected they feel and whether they feel that their voices are valued
* Offer support by sharing a story of how you are trying to leverage a strength from the previous list for the betterment of the team and to achieve your shared goals
* Try to help them make a connection to one of the listed strengths that is important for them to feel included and engaged with the team

You may encounter situations with individuals who act in complete contrast to these inclusive behaviors and they will be the most challenging. Yet, this is an important test of your ability to transform the organization, because people who do desire the same equality and inclusivity as you are watching to see who will back down and who will strive to take steps forward.

As you build allies in this effort to grow the team's appreciation for working in an inclusive environment that values all perspectives and backgrounds, you will start to feel momentum for the changes you want to ignite. Warning: Leading transformation has the power to become infectious!

Take Control of Your Growth and Development

Preparing yourself to lead others while remaining focused on your own goals is filled with many challenges and opportunities for personal growth. Your career in your twenties and early thirties is a roller coaster, particularly as you navigate what you really want out of work AND life. You make mistakes, you shake them off, you try again, and you keep putting yourself out there for the next opportunity, building toward the chance to formally lead. Then, all of a sudden, you are a manager accountable for others' performance.

In the United States, the average age we become managers is thirty years old, but the average age we receive leadership training is forty-five. So guess what? There won't be a play-book waiting for you when you arrive. How do you handle challenges with a direct report? How do you hold conversations about pay raises or the lack thereof, develop yourself while you are accountable for developing others, or master your own calendar while making time for regular check-ins with your team? The following real-world advice about how to take control of your growth and development derives from the thir-teen years I spent in the pharmaceutical industry, and my experiences as an entrepreneur and as a coach and mentor to thousands of women at every stage in their career.

In my previous book, *Misunderstood Millennial Talent: The Other 91%,* I unveiled the deficit of investment in millennial employees, citing about $1,200 per person. Companies in many cases spend more money on an employee's computer than on her growth and development! Motherhood is not the primary reason women around thirty are leaving organizations. These women rank pay, lack of learning and development, and a shortage of meaningful work as the primary reasons why they leave organizations. For women in the first decade of their career, I see a critical opportunity to pursue develop-mental roles and experiences that will stretch their skills, knowledge, and context so that they can thrive in the next decade instead of opting out. In the majority of research studies

I audited and led, women reported having a weaker external network than their male colleagues. And, quite often and disturbingly, companies discourage women and younger employees from attending external conferences where they could broaden their network within their industry and beyond. I once tried to pursue membership for my company with an industry-sponsored women's organization, only to be told by both a female and a male executive that "we don't pay for our women to network and seek out better job opportunities elsewhere." Wow, that said it all to me. I knew firsthand this was not a common sentiment by leaders, since my previous employer had consistently offered and sponsored external learning and networking opportunities. This illustrates the difference between leaders and companies who understand the power of developing positive ambassadors versus those who operate in fear of supporting their employee's growth.

If you're going to dig your heels in, you have to be proactive about your own growth and development. Every year, organizations carve out a finite piece of their budgets to invest in high-potential training and development programs aimed at "building the bench" of future leaders. A high potential (HiPo) is an individual with the ability, aspiration, and engagement to rise to and succeed in more senior, critical positions. Savvy corporate leaders support early-career HiPos by giving them opportunities to move among different company divisions and by offering enhanced training and development, executive coaching, and senior executive sponsorship. Many programs focused solely on women are on the rise, but the nomination and selection process can feel elusive.

I do want to emphasize that budgets for training are not always available for everyone and not every company will offer it. You must be your number one career advocate and take responsibility for growing your knowledge and skills independent of company resources. Managing oneself as overall process was presented to us by Peter F. Drucker in his study "Managing Oneself," which was published in *Harvard Business Review* in 1999. We have to place ourselves where we can make the greatest contribution to our organizations and communities. And we have to stay mentally alert and engaged, which means knowing how and when to change the work that we do. Drucker raised the most important questions you have to answer. "What are my strengths?" "How do I perform?" "What are my values?" "Where do I belong?" This is a great place to start your own reflections.[3]

I suggest learning as much as you can about how your company invests in leadership development (for nonmanagers and managers), then setting up coffee meetings with someone in HR and potential mentors in various parts of the organization who have advanced to higher leadership levels. The goal is to ask questions and express your interest in and dedication to growing as a leader within the organization. You do want to make sure you have this proactive and ongoing discussion with your manager but gathering insight and ideas from various perspectives will help you identify the training pathways and development you want to pursue.

Depending on the size of your company, HR may not have formal programs in-house, but you can hope that it will be willing to sponsor the fee or be flexible with your hours in order for you to attend a conference or local training program, or to participate in an external professional group. Come prepared for your meeting with HR to discuss these options, focusing on the "what's in it for the company" angle.

The one approach I always recommend to young women is to volunteer and devote time on nonprofit boards because, for one thing, these boards need and are hugely appreciative of your service, and, for another, you will have the chance to lead and take on broader responsibilities than are typically available to you at that early stage of your career and that will stretch and grow your skills.

When I was twenty-one years old, I earned a junior board position with Girls Hope of Pittsburgh, an organization that helps young women build a foundation for success by providing them a nurturing home, quality education, and opportunities through college. It was a meaningful and rewarding experience for me because I was exposed to women and men who were senior leaders in industries outside my own (health care). More important, the volunteer work with girls was inspiring on many levels.

But I made one huge mistake that haunted me for quite some time. I had a big idea for a Girls Hope fundraiser that was completely out of the box and would require a pretty significant effort to pull off (resources, staffing, and sponsorship). The senior board approved my idea and gave me the reins to make it happen. I was thrilled to share this opportunity back at my job with my then manager, but was completely devastated when he dismissed it as something unrelated to my day job that could distract from my work goals.

At that point, I felt that I was giving my all to my job, working from 7 a.m. to 7 p.m. most days of the week and taking on evening and weekend client events, as I was the only person on my team who was single and without children. Despite my frustration, I soldiered on, putting a ton of energy into pulling off this huge fundraiser, burning the candle at both ends. In the process of building and launching my dream event, I made a big administrative mistake at work that caused a chain reaction of negative events.

Ultimately, my company acknowledged that I had always had good intentions and that it was a genuine mistake. But it cast a negative light on my external commitments, which I perceived as instrumental to my engagement and advancement. As a result of my error, my manager discouraged me from taking on these external time commitments as well as from pursuing my MBA with company sponsorship.

Looking back, I wish I had approached the conversation with my manager about this community leadership role as a negotiation, with a timeline, a plan for how I would stay on top of my responsibilities, and a clear connection to how this volunteer role would improve my performance at work and benefit the company overall. I could have pressed for a broader discussion comparing this area of focus to those of others on the team. Maybe then my boss would have gotten on board and helped me evaluate options for time management and sharing responsibilities with my colleagues. (This approach also could have saved me a great deal of money, considering that once I did decide to pursue my MBA, I had to attend at night, paid for it predominantly on my own, and it took six years to earn my degree.)

So here's my advice to you: Map out the developmental opportunities you believe are worth your time, and proactively discuss them with your direct leaders so that they understand what the benefit will be both to you and to the company. I would even set up meetings with a contact in HR to keep her or him in the loop on the progress of your initiative for self-development. Learn from my mistake and be prepared in advance to prove your ability to handle multiple commitments, and keep everyone updated along the way.

The following are a number of other self-led areas of growth and development that I believe are critical for young women to explore:

* Stretch assignments outside your core pathway and direct responsibilities
* 360 feedback assessments with constructive and actionable feedback (more on this in chapter 6)
* Increase your knowledge and awareness of stakeholder management (aim to understand who's who across all leadership roles and business functions to get a stronger understanding of how everyone works together to achieve the larger business goals)
* Profit and loss (P&L) responsibility
* Overseas assignments
* Global business responsibilities
* Board of director experience (nonprofit, alumni/academic, or at start-ups)
* Internal early-career professional networks or local organizations focused on connecting young professionals (join, or launch your own)
* Negotiation skills (for yourself and as an advocate for the employees you lead)
* Shadow experiences (shadowing senior executives to increase your exposure, raise your visibility, and expand your context)

During the last year of my MBA program at Rutgers University, I gained approval from my company to attend a two-week educational immersion program in China. This was the year of the Beijing Olympics, and because I had not had the opportunity to study abroad during my undergraduate years, I was very excited about this experience. I also saw this as a chance to increase exposure for my company's global business operations and connect with the affiliate leaders in Shanghai and Beijing.

There was no clear pathway for me to pursue this idea of connecting with my company's Shanghai office, and my direct leadership didn't have any connections. So I started sending emails to colleagues in different departments in hopes that someone could make me an introduction to someone in the Shanghai office. Finally, I struck gold: A marketing peer knew two senior leaders there. I reviewed the organization chart for our internal network and familiarized myself with their background so that I could craft a more personalized note. Fast forward: I was able to visit the office for the day and meet with several counterparts in sales and marketing who shared a similar area of business priorities, so we could exchange ideas and experiences.

What was most memorable was going to lunch with a woman my age who was also completing her MBA and had similar career aspirations. We talked about work and life goals, and it was truly remarkable how much we had in common, from challenges and disappointments to results and rewards.

My takeaway: Don't expect someone else to take your career growth by the reins. Think outside the box and leverage any and every opportunity you have to develop yourself, your network, and your exposure to potential pathways.

Engage Your Employee Women's Network

Women's employee resource groups or networks are an underestimated engine for fueling wide-scale change and tangible momentum in our mission for equality. Employee resource groups (ERGs)—voluntary, employee-led groups made up of individuals who join based on common interests, backgrounds, or demographic factors such as gender, race, or ethnicity—have been around for decades and currently exist at 90 percent of Fortune 500 companies.[4] They aim to foster a diverse, inclusive workplace aligned to a company's mission, values, goals, business practices, and objectives. The benefits include the development of future leaders, increased employee engagement, and expanded marketplace reach stemming from the efforts to leverage diverse employee insights.

In recent years, ERGs have been proven to enable change at all levels, complementing senior leadership–driven diversity and inclusion strategies within organizations. A 2017 study found that 86 percent of female respondents believe that participating in their corporate women's ERGs specifically benefited them and their career.[5] Over two-thirds of those respondents said that their women's ERG had actually helped create policy changes at work.

Let's assume you are already involved in your women's network, so now the big bold move is to determine how you can add value to lead the charge for change within your organization. In the introduction, I mentioned the engagement that had the greatest impact on me, the Women's Employee Journey commissioned by Lilly. It explored the experiences of female employees of all ages and levels in the organization to better support them and achieve gender parity. The Lilly

Women's Employee Journey identified real and tangible barriers that inhibit women from bringing their whole selves to work, from being heard, from realizing their full potential, and from advancing in their careers and into key decision-making roles.

Your network can seek out a more intimate understanding of the experiences of women working at your company to better identify where you can begin to remove barriers and formulate your own solutions.

I can't emphasize enough how critical it is for your network to ensure that colleagues do not perceive it as an exclusive club. Your women's network must be a true community that works together (with women and men) to make an organization evolve to the level we all deserve. We need you to look out for one another, to build this community of true support and alliance knowing that first we must overcome these barriers for ourselves, and then we can do it for our colleagues, our friends, our protégés, our daughters, and our sons.

Amanda Apodaca has been a leader in the Women's Initiative for Leading at Lilly (WILL, mentioned in the introduction) since its inception; she leads WILL's company-wide advocacy program, a multilevel development initiative created to embolden women and men to speak up and lead change in their respective business divisions. Amanda's "why" for leading WILL and advocating for gender equality is very personal. It stems from the journey her son has been on since he was diagnosed at age three with apraxia, a neurological condition similar to what a stroke victim deals with. For people with apraxia, their brain can't tell their mouths the right shapes to make in order to form intelligible speech.

Amanda proactively shares with her colleagues and others how her family's emotional and educational experience has strengthened her convictions about the power of a women's network. The efforts she leads to develop advocates who help others connect their personal experiences to their day-to-day interactions (with colleagues, customers, and executives) result in extraordinary business outcomes and elevated employee engagement.

> Early on, WILL realized that advocacy would be an essential component of driving change. It is critical that each of us has a clear understanding of what fuels our passion for achieving gender equality at our company and the personal role that we're willing to play in advocating more boldly and more often than we have in the past. Because here is the thing: I don't just have a son; I also have a daughter who at some point will be entering the workforce and was put on this earth to accomplish amazing things.

The keys to the success of a women's network in driving change are its principles and its people. You need to agree on guiding principles around which you can organize your people, processes, and programs. Creating a governance structure that is inclusive but also flexible gives you the space to adapt as the organization's goals expand and you learn more about what women at your company need. You have to be clear about short-term or year 1 goals as well as long-term, three-plus-year goals to demonstrate a solid intention to impact on your organization's systems and leadership practices.

I learned a great deal from WILL's founding chair, Laurie Kowalevsky, about conceiving the network's strategy in the way one would a global brand launch (for example, the logo, the internal and external messages, the various stakeholder engagement strategies, thinking big about resources, and the collective ability to scale to be available to women in all parts of the organization), to help you develop highly specific plans and determine how much help you will need. A clear brand and strategy for your women's network will illustrate the broad impact for the organization and increase support by executive leadership so it can be seen as a top-three business priority.

The biggest takeaway for me was to secure the highest level of executive sponsorship. It's not typical for the CEO to be an ERG sponsor, but a member of the executive committee (those directly reporting to the CEO) should be. This sponsor should be visible, actively involved, and heavily invested in the impact and outcomes. He or she should have regular interaction with your leadership team and be present at key events. For a more detailed guide on launching, reinventing, and mobilizing your women's network for its greatest impact, see the Resources section in the chapter 4 summary at the end of the book.

ERGs are not just good for business; they are essential to your company's future. Commit to growing the impact of your women's network. You can help build up the talent pipeline of women and foster relationships and a stronger sense of belonging and community, while also demonstrating the clear alignment of diversity initiatives with business interests.

Lift as You Climb

Paying it forward by intentionally devoting time to mentoring younger women is absolutely critical to creating change within the business world. Even in the earliest stages of your career, it is possible (and beneficial) for you to be a strong role model for girls and women who will follow in your footsteps. Making time for mentoring will nourish your spirit and remind you of the larger impact made possible through your individual success.

We women tend to underestimate our own abilities and attribute our success to external factors such as "getting lucky" or "help from others." We must change this pattern by modeling the ability to take credit for our own efforts and hard work; as a role model and mentor, you can proudly share your accomplishments to help our next generation internalize their own dreams and to inspire their self-confidence. When girls see that it is okay to own their success, they will feel more comfortable pursuing it. For the leaders reading this chapter, it is important to inform yourself about models for formal mentoring across the company and forge successful partnerships with community organizations where female leaders can extend their impact to students.

One of the many significant memories of my experiences as a mentor to younger women through community-based organizations was participating in "Hot Jobs, Cool Women", a program targeted at the Young Women's Leadership Schools. Whenever I showed up to speak to a class of high school girls (usually all girls of color from underserved communities), I remember being intimidated by their confidence and tremendously inspired by who they were determined to be in their lives. They were so brave and focused, which in turn helped me find my own courage to dream bigger. The impact was not one way; it was mutually beneficial for all of us. Talking about my career and life path with these young women—not to draw insignificant parallels but to share the insights I had gathered in my journey that could help them grow faster and become something bigger than they could imagine—was a humbling experience.

Mentorship is critically important. Too many working professionals feel that they don't have the time to be a mentor, but you have to make the time. Treat mentoring as a vital activity in your life because if you don't, you are not only missing out on an opportunity to help yourself but also denying the next generation an opportunity to help them be better and do better.

I'm proud to be a board member for Girls Inc. of New York City. Girls Inc. is a national nonprofit organization that focuses on empowering, coaching, and building mentoring relationships with girls across the US. We offer in-school and after-school intentional programming that covers a wide range of topics that affect girls today and inspires them to be strong, smart, and bold. Our newest initiative, Teen Leadership Circles, provides an intensive, gender-specific training and development program for high school girls. Young women are trained to become peer leaders who can educate and support their peers by creating girls-only safe spaces and facilitating workshops. Our goal is to inspire young women to become advocates who positively influence their peers and ultimately change the world.

It's important to note that your role in uplifting other women isn't limited only to working with those who are more junior than you. Champion your peers and the women leaders who inspire you! Strive to be the type of leader who provides honest feedback in a way that is intended to empower and help someone achieve her potential. Be an advocate for the women on your team, in your department, and in the executive offices to demonstrate the pride you have in their work.

Ignite an Industry-Wide Conversation

The conversation about achieving gender parity and building a more inclusive workplace culture is one that everyone in your organization (and industry) needs to be having, not just women. Make your voice heard about the importance of different styles of leadership, flexible work options, and diverse paths up the corporate ladder that can contribute to the success of the company. Arm yourself with The Business Case for Change (see the end of the book) to encourage employees from different levels and backgrounds and with diverse work and life needs to get on board. That's what Ashley Batson, executive director of the South Carolina (SC) Asphalt Pavement Association, is doing for the male-dominated asphalt industry through the group she cofounded, Women of Asphalt.

The stated goals of Women of Asphalt are to foster and promote mentoring and networking opportunities; create professional development opportunities through education and training; advocate for women; and encourage other women to join the asphalt industry. Ashley and Women of Asphalt have ignited an industry-wide conversation around the importance of women to the asphalt industry and the issues they face in the field, such as being taken seriously when dealing with a crew of men, how not to come on too strong but also assert their authority, portraying themselves strongly, communicating well, and being respected.

The first big Women of Asphalt event was held with a packed house of almost 150 men and women who participated in in-depth discussions about the status of the industry in terms of workforce and the need to recruit women. The members of

Women of Asphalt are adamant that both men and women need to be on board with the changes the group is pushing forward—everyone must bring in all the talent he or she can. The group understands that industry-wide awareness is the first step to acknowledging there is a problem and then solving it.

Find ways to bring up the case for change in a positive, benefits-driven way whenever possible. Seek out the people who are on board with effecting change, to amplify your voice and spark a movement toward creating a more inclusive workplace. Reach out to peers in different teams or to colleagues with whom you have personal relationships, to involve them in this broader conversation. Together you can establish shared goals, experiment with intentional behaviors, and prescribe ways to keep each other accountable.

You can begin by scheduling a meeting with someone in one of the following key stakeholder groups who should be invested in this discussion:

* D&I team
* HR analytics team
* HR recruitment team

The individuals in these roles have access to information from employees and about employees that sheds light on the urgency of improving gender representation and the inclusion of diverse voices. Share with them your own example of how you diagnosed your behavior (first big bold move) and the impact that those who model inclusive behaviors have on your team. Be candid about the successes or challenges you have encountered and come prepared with ideas for where you see an opportunity for the company to grow. Your work in the "Diagnosing Your Company Culture" section in chapter 2 is a strong start in breaking down the culture dynamics that hold women back from advancing. Maybe there is a need for training in identifying and dismantling unconscious bias, an internal communication campaign around stronger standards for inclusive behaviors at work, or resources to guide team building that clearly address gender bias.

As you work to expand the number of allies in this effort, some big questions will arise:

* How can we hold leaders accountable and improve the communication skills of managers, particularly those who exhibit gender bias and use language derogatory to women?
* How can our company integrate inclusive leadership practice into learning and development plans and performance management processes? How do we reward and recognize success, and even penalize actions that don't measure up?
* How important is this effort to your senior leadership team?

These are the key questions that Laura Gentile and Alison Overholt, two of the leading female executives at ESPN, considered as they embarked on a mission to transform the beloved brand and traditional employer into one that could attract women and diverse talent of all ages. They are responsible for creating lasting change in a male-dominated industry. Laura ideated and launched espnW and now holds the position of senior vice president for business operations and content strategy. Alison serves as vice president of espnW as well as editor-in-chief of *ESPN The Magazine*—the first woman in this role at a major US sports magazine.

Women make up 49 percent of all sports fans, and eighty million women consume ESPN every month. Laura and Alison understand that women are a key demographic for the success and growth of the sports industry. Research shows that 45 percent of millennial sports fans are women, yet the sports industry continues to be a male-dominated arena that creates barriers for women entering the industry and advancing to leadership positions.[6] In spring 2016, espnW visited twelve colleges and met with two thousand female student-athletes. These "campus conversations" gave young female athletes a forum to discuss their unique issues and built a bridge for the industry to strengthen its female numbers and increase funding for more female-centered initiatives.

Holly Lindvall is the vice president for human resources and diversity at the New York Mets baseball organization and a passionate champion for women in the sports industry. Holly supports the Women's Sports Foundation, which was founded by tennis legend Billie Jean King. The foundation is dedicated to creating leaders by ensuring all girls have access to sports. Using her insider perspective in the industry and role in human resources, she devotes time to mentor and advise female athletes as they are transitioning from playing sports to the world of work—whether graduating or retiring.

> Through workshops at various college campuses all across the country, I have been able to connect with strong women and talk about openings in my company. I have to fit this in outside of my daily responsibilities but the women we have hired inspire me to keep going! They are outside of our traditional recruiting networks but I know that they broaden the range of diversity in gender, age, race, and skill set for our business. In my first workshop for the Women's Sports Foundation, I met Sydni. She was finishing her last year in her graduate program while continuing to compete on the basketball

court. She did not have time to do traditional internships outside of the demands of her sports schedule and therefore [felt] insecure about the next steps in her career journey as she approached graduation. I stayed after my presentation to talk to her one-on-one and we made an immediate connection. I admired her drive. We continued the conversation throughout her last year of school on the phone and regular emails. We hired her as an intern and then a full-time employee into our community engagement department. She brings her teamwork, ability to take feedback, and time management skills from the court to the office.

You need to make time for networking to help generate positive momentum for recruiting and engaging women in any industry. Focus on the quality of the connections over the quantity and connect with woman at all stages throughout their journey from campus to career. Reach out through networks that exist or initiate your own. Start by building awareness and creating a company-wide conversation. Then you can expand industry wide to share the commitment to a more diverse workforce and an equal voice for women at every intersection where women in your business can connect.

Accelerate toward Equal Representation

When you can see women who look like you in positions you aspire to hold—in your field of work, at your company's highest levels, and in your community, daily communications, and yes, your country—your confidence that you can reach those heights yourself grows. This message is a thread throughout this book and everything I believe we need to work toward. It's not enough that women make up more than half the workforce; we need to have access to and hold positions at the highest levels of every organization, community, and nation. So what can you do? Start with your own team and create specific goals for achieving 50-50 representation of women.

JP Morgan Chase Women on the Move is a global, firm-wide initiative that empowers female employees, clients, and consumers to build their careers, grow their businesses, and improve their financial health. Women on the Move is led by Samantha Saperstein and backed by the firm's leadership team and operating committee—half of whom are women. One of the three focus areas is to propel women into leadership positions across the firm. This example and several others, such as EY Fast Forward and The CEO Action for Diversity and Inclusion, are global programs that are worth looking into as models to inspire your own efforts within your company. Reach out to the individuals leading these efforts and mentioned in their press releases to learn more and how to collaborate.

If you are the team leader, become more intentional about succession planning and recruiting. Discuss this goal with your team and engage their support and accountability. If you are an individual contributor, meet with your manager and explicitly state that equal representation is an important value to you (citing all the stats I provide in The Business Case for Change section at the end of the book), and offer to help. Ask your manager where he or she sees the opportunity to involve more women in your direct work and how you can help leadership expose more women to your team, department, and company. You can also play a huge role in the recruitment and outreach to qualified women who could join your company.

Through the consulting work I have led with our clients at Columbia Business School and the University of North Carolina Kenan-Flagler Business School, we've learned that women must be engaged much earlier in their lives to expose them to the benefits of an MBA. These efforts are critical to helping women believe that business school is a viable, accessible opportunity for them. The goals are to increase the female application pool and enrollment to grow the number of female MBA graduates ready to lead organizations around the world.

Get Pay Straight

Shonda Rhimes, producer, screenwriter, and author, shared the following:

> I am the highest-paid showrunner in television . . . The other day I came to this conclusion that men brag and women hide. Even when they don't deserve to brag, men brag . . . and when men do deserve to brag, they are good at it. When Ryan [Murphy] made his amazing deal with Netflix, what did he do? He shouted his salary to the world and he did this gorgeous cover shoot and photo for *The Hollywood Reporter* and he deserved every minute of it. I applaud him. . . . When I made a deal with Netflix, I let them report my salary wrong in the press, and then I did as few interviews as possible and I put my head down and worked. In other words, I hid. I'm getting this award [*Elle Magazine*'s twenty-fifth annual women in Hollywood celebration] for inspiring other women—how can I inspire anyone if I'm hiding?

One of the most high-impact areas for change in US companies is gender wage equity. In the United States, the average woman still makes just 77 cents to the male dollar over their lifetimes—and even less if she's a woman of color. There is controversy around these numbers, yet even when you compare apples to apples—for example, MBA grads one year out of business school and working in the same jobs—women still earn just 93 percent of what men do.[7] So how do you know whether gender pay equity is affecting you personally, and what can you do about it?

It is a fact that when women negotiate for better pay, they're often perceived as "pushy" and are less likely to get the raise than men doing the same thing. In the 2017 McKinsey and Lean In study of top firms in the US, researchers found that women who negotiated were 67 percent more likely to receive feedback that their personal style was "intimidating" or "too aggressive."[8] Yet we can't let this hold us back from asking for more. We need to encourage women to speak up and keep asking for what they are worth on being hired and every step along their career journey. We must research an employer and the industry to try to uncover the pay ranges for the skills and expertise women could bring to the role. If we come to these discussions well informed and prepared to be as specific as possible, we can more clearly advocate for what we want and deserve.

Let's begin with assessing your true worth and market value. Please know that this is not the salary.com way, which you can use as a starting point but which will not give you a thorough assessment of your breadth of experience, education, and role responsibilities. You must map out all these pieces yourself and list out your pay along with benefits to be firm in preparing to negotiate tactfully and effectively.

The typical advice for negotiation is not at all relevant for individuals in a corporate setting where there are annual reviews, pay scales, and department caps on wage increases. You need to do some legwork to understand how financial rewards are calculated and distributed in your company. This requires reading anything made available to you at your current level, scheduling an appointment with HR, and engaging in open discussions with your manager. You may find the thought of such efforts stressful or frightening, but you have to break the cycle and initiate these conversations.

If it makes you feel more comfortable, think about these initial discussions as regarding company compensation processes and not your specific situation. To gain a stronger understanding of how your chosen career path will affect your pay, you want to learn as much as you can about the impact of level, department, and tenure on pay and benefits. Putting together all the facts about your own compensation (what you are paid and what you believe the compensation should be for your level and productivity, given your company's policies) will put you in the driver's seat for a direct conversation about pursuing an increase.

Advocate Behind Closed Doors

When are key decisions made about "who has potential," "who gets promoted," and "who is not ready"? In talent management discussions and formal performance reviews. Typically, HR and the management team are present with a senior leader, and these meetings are a regular occurrence at the larger, more traditional organizations.

Our big goal as women is to get in that room. Earn a seat at the table by becoming a manager or a key maker of talent decisions in your organization. Then you can be a strong advocate for ensuring that these discussions are conducted with a balance of men and women with equal voice in decisions having to do with promotions and people's potential.

A challenging aspect of these company meetings is that they can focus too much on past performance and technical skills and are based solely on manager nominations (which can be contaminated by politics and vague arm's-length observations). As a result, the typical HiPo assessment of who has what it takes to advance looks a lot like a popularity contest. You need to have an advocate behind closed doors because that's where the fate of your career may matter most.

Our second goal is to help our employers recognize that traditional gender stereotypes that over-associate career ambition with men, and flexibility and work-life balance with women are starkly out of date and detrimental to a diverse talent pool.

The third goal, a more personal one, is for you to gain clarity and gather details on your company's approach to talent identification overall. Do you know the process and timeline for these types of discussions at your company? Do they change as you rise in the ranks or by department? A CEO once shared with me that over the course of one month, all the one-on-one discussions he had with male employees centered around the knowledge they had about upcoming talent sessions. Each man who met with the CEO was positioning himself, providing accounts of all his results and career interests in advance. Not one of the female employees who came into his office for a one-on-one even had a clue that these sessions were approaching, nor did they come prepared to advocate for their own potential. He was in disbelief that the men seemed more informed and aware of the talent process than any of the women. As a result, he was determined to address it company wide and ensure the talent management system overall was transparent and accessible to all employees. That's advocacy in action from the very top.

You must understand the talent process, the timeline, and the "who's who" in the room. The impact of those decisions and discussions will help you identify the people who need to get to know you, your performance, and your potential. This knowledge of the entire ecosystem that affects advancement and promotion will become an important asset in your career planning and your road map for whom you must build relationships with.

* * *

Being brave and pursuing bold moves is core to the "Dig Your Heels In" philosophy. I encourage you to use them however they serve your life and career goals. It doesn't matter which move you make or in which order; what matters is that you do something. Right now, choose one move that you will invest time in over the next month. Once you begin to follow the advice and put the ideas into action, I suspect that the momentum will take over, and you will feel the urgency to continue digging.

Overcoming Obstacles

In this chapter, you will learn about the common self-limiting behaviors that hold women back and the strategies to overcome them:
* Imposter syndrome
* Stifled authenticity
* The myth of meritocracy
* Good-girl thinking

Unconscious or implicit biases are "social stereotypes about certain groups of people that individuals form outside their own conscious awareness."[1] Everyone holds unconscious beliefs about different groups, even the groups to which she herself belongs! When you define yourself or are defined by others along these narrow lines, it's like being in a cage, unable to break through and be your true self and reach your true potential. In the corporate world, the unconscious biases against women that you encounter on a day-to-day basis can reinforce self-limiting behaviors and decisions about whether you can bring your whole self to work and have an equal opportunity to contribute and succeed. I've learned to recognize when these obstacles are most damaging to a woman's career from the interviews, focus groups, and surveys I've facilitated, where women of all ages (e.g., MBA students, mid-level managers, and executive leaders) have shared the key tensions that arise in their career journey. The four in this chapter are the common obstacles that women face and a battle plan for taking back our power follows each obstacle.

Imposter Syndrome

The only way you get what you want is by asking for it and having the courage to take it once you get it. So there are times when you have to ask for that added responsibility and times when you have to just take that opportunity to lead. You are never going to get it if you sit back and continually say and believe, "I don't have it."

In regards to gender issues, I act no differently today than I acted when I was an associate twenty years ago. I believed I could change just as much then as I believe I can change now. Some would say I was or maybe still am naïve, but that was really how it is with me. Because to me, believing that being a girl in some way made me not as skilled as "the boys" was just not acceptable. And no one was going to change that in me, even if a few tried. It was in my fabric, and some things about your fabric just do not change regardless of your job, company, boss, or level. I give my parents a lot of credit for that.

—Michelle Carnahan, North America Head of Diabetes and Cardiovascular for Sanofi

Have you ever felt as though you just weren't good enough to apply for a position, despite really wanting it? Do you ever second-guess yourself before you walk into a big meeting or a presentation, feeling as though you don't have what it takes to be in the room? You are not alone: 70 percent of us experience imposter syndrome at some point in our careers.[2]

"Imposters" suffer from chronic self-doubt that overrides any external proof of their competence. They feel inadequate, despite having evidence of their success. It's a phenomenon that touches everyone, even high-achieving, highly successful people, and is not equated with low self-esteem or a lack of self-confidence. Some researchers have linked it with perfectionism, especially in women.

Imposter syndrome can strike at any moment. The most common reaction for women is to avoid self-promotion for fear of being called out, an obvious barrier to career growth. Some women hide their achievements through their focus on communal leadership, attributing success to teamwork or luck, effectively removing their individual effort from the table.

This decreased visibility can lead to a recurring disbelief in your skills and, consequently, perfectionism and an excessive focus on impression management.[3] Women with imposter syndrome often feel that they have to master their current level before they can take on new responsibilities or be seen as ready for the next level. By contrast, men often feel comfortable jumping into new opportunities, regardless of whether they meet the requirements of the position.

As a contributor for ForbesWomen media, I was given the opportunity to interview Reese Witherspoon, award-winning actress, producer, author, and entrepreneur. Reese is a bold, impressive leader with a mile-long list of accomplishments and a strong legacy of success and positive impact, yet even she deals with bouts of imposter syndrome daily. When those moments strike, she channels the advice from her good friend Mindy Kaling, whose book *Why Not Me?* pushes her to re-evaluate why she should doubt her worthiness or credibility. I can picture the audio track in Reese's mind: *"Why shouldn't I be in the room with those studio executives making key decisions? Why shouldn't I have a place at the table when we discuss retail operations or business objectives when I am closest to our target customers because I am those women?"*

Reese also confided to me that even though she has found a mechanism to snap herself out of feeling like an imposter and instead power through, there have been situations where it got the best of her, and she either abandoned or delayed the pursuit of something she wanted for herself professionally. Can you relate?

Strategy 1: Own Your Success

The women I interviewed who battled moments of imposter syndrome said they intentionally made the time to fully understand the unique value they brought to their jobs. Follow this advice and spend time reflecting on how you see yourself. Self-awareness is the first step to owning your power.

Develop an "own your success" mentality by documenting and digesting your accomplishments. I want you to create a "for your eyes only" list of your successes in a journal, on your computer, or anywhere that you feel comfortable. Don't waste time making it pretty or perfect—just start writing! Later on, you can reference this list when making network connections and perfecting your personal pitch.

I recommend reviewing your achievements list every day for ten days. Pay attention to what comes up for you. Are you inspired to add more to the list as you reflect on the many ways you have had an impact? Are you getting clearer on what your personal brand is and what value you bring to your organization? What are your unique skills that thread through each of these accomplishments?

Battling imposter syndrome isn't about gaining new skills; it's about acknowledging and being proud of the skills and achievements you already have. By establishing a habit of reflecting on the accomplishments you are proud of, you will waste less time on negative, disempowering thoughts. When you truly believe in your value, when you own it, you can confidently express it, just as Vartika Prasad did.

Vartika Prasad became a partner with PwC in New York City, one of the early ones from her background to achieve that milestone. She credits her achievement to her journey of immigrating to the United States from India, learning to navigate a new culture without losing belief in her capabilities, and maintaining her authenticity amid forces of change. She launched her career with PwC in India and had five years in audit under her belt when she decided to move to New York City. Although there wasn't a job opening for her at that specific time, she took the risk and moved on her own, continuing to pursue ways to keep herself active in the profession. Within a year of her move, Vartika had secured that spot with PwC in New York City, but she also had to hold firm to her previous tenure to ensure it was applied to her new position.

Certain things that you think should be automatic are not actually so and need a deliberate action from one's side. I made sure that my previous tenure of service in India was carried over to the US. That impacts your resume considerably; it impacts your years of service, your benefits, and your promotions. I coach people that you've got to ask for it and not assume it will happen on its own.

During the early years of her US career, Vartika realized

so much of it was doing everything all over again to prove yourself, while already having proved yourself well in another country and another environment. I empathize with those changing roles, jobs, countries, because not only do you have to prove yourself generally, but you have to prove that you are ready to be given responsibility to make decisions and lead people. It's one thing to re-establish yourself in the workplace, but it's even harder to get there and say, "Hey, I can lead you."

Strategy 2: Reframe the Negative

The next time the feeling arises that you are not enough, *write it down.* Push yourself to actually type or spell out the feelings that are holding you back. Right beside where you have written out that moment, write down an accurate, realistic assessment of your performance to combat that mind-set. Learn to reframe the negative assessment and disempowering thoughts into a positive affirmation by using an encouraging outlook. It takes practice to learn not to dwell. Build this habit so that you can counter that inner critic as soon as it rears its ugly head.

Here is how Vartika reframes her negative thoughts:

* **Identify whether you are comparing yourself to an existing norm.** Are you feeling incapable just because you

don't fit that norm? Is this really a norm everyone should adhere to? Is there a better way to think about this?

* **Evaluate whether your thoughts are clouded by an unfair comparison.** Is there any evidence to support your thoughts? Is your judgment just being clouded by stereotypes?
* **Reaffirm your unique strengths.** Become aware of what you bring to the table independent of that norm. Don't let your inner critic, with its irrational comparisons, be in charge.

Strategy 3: Call a Friend

I'll repeat this advice over and over throughout the book because relationships make a huge difference, not just for your personal life but for your career. (That's why I dedicated an entire chapter to the topic!) You have to find people, several if possible, to whom you can reach out when you need a sounding board. Text a mentor: "I have a tough situation at work and I'd love your advice." If you first work through it on paper and in your head, then you will be a lot clearer and more succinct when asking someone else for her insight.

Sometimes all we need is a boost of energy and positive reinforcement to help us get through. Other times we need to hear someone we respect remind us of our strengths, assure us that "this too shall pass," and encourage us to stick it out. Author and the *New York Times*'s first gender editor, Jessica Bennett, provides numerous strategies to help women push back on gender-biased and self-limiting behaviors including this great advice, "If you hear an idea from a woman that you think is good, back her up. You'll have more of an effect than you think and you'll establish yourself as a team player too."[4]

Join a Lean In Circle, connect through Bumble, attend a local chamber of commerce event, or reconnect with your alma mater's alumni association. You don't have to go at this alone. And even if you feel that you have a good number of people in your corner, continue to grow your network and expand your own availability to people who could use a trustworthy source of advice.

Stifled Authenticity

Women walk a tightrope to make others feel comfortable with their gender and style. But when you believe you need to change yourself in some way to fit in, then you lose your ability to lead authentically. The pressure for women to conform exists at all levels, but particularly as we advance to higher levels of leadership where there is a common male archetype. Some companies are making progress with women holding leadership roles all the way up through their highest levels of seniority, but most have not yet gotten comfortable with a feminine style of leadership—which, by the way, could be embodied by both men and women. The result is that although women may be prepared to put themselves in a position to succeed, they'd rather think about leaving an organization than have to change who they are to get ahead.

Strategy 4: Cultivate Your Personal Brand and Advocate for It

Cultivating your personal brand can help you stay true to who you are when a situation becomes challenging. The first step in developing and owning your personal brand is to identify your natural strengths that bring you the most energy. Reflect on the list you began for Strategy 1 and pull out the skills that contributed to each of your successes. Interesting note: Research shows that it is better to spend your time and energy leveraging and developing existing strengths than it is trying to correct a weakness.[5] The takeaway? Leveraging your natural strengths and allowing your true self to shine through will ultimately get you further than trying to be someone you are not. This is something Jennifer Schubach learned over time in her career in the pharmaceutical industry.

Jennifer has worked in the pharmaceutical industry for more than fifteen years and is currently director of oncology at Pfizer. In the first half of her career, she felt pressure to conform to a more traditional, buttoned-up style of leadership. How she spoke, dressed, and behaved was largely influenced by what she thought others expected of her.

> Something shifted about five years ago that helped my authentic self shine through, partly because I gained more confidence in my abilities and also as I achieved more seniority. And, quite frankly, also because it was exhausting. Exhausting to always feel that you have to act differently and be someone that wasn't natural to my style. What I realize now is that my sense of humor, my dry candor and approach are what make me unique and memorable. There was a situation around that time where I was presenting at a very senior leadership meeting on a tense and highly sensitive situation. I made a joke at a key moment, and it helped diffuse the tension, and ultimately everyone had space to laugh, relax, and refocus.

After that meeting, key leaders remembered her and that moment—not just because she was funny but because she became someone who stood out. She had command of the data and the information, but also the confidence to pivot and lighten the mood to engage everyone without losing her credibility.

Jennifer's ability to use her skill in getting people together is now an asset on the job. She can bring groups of people to a better place and use her skills to make stronger one-on-one connections.

Strategy 5: Speak Up

Authenticity relies on the courage to stand up and be yourself. We owe it to ourselves and our colleagues to bring our true selves to work. Cultivating authenticity requires personal reflection on your core values and beliefs. It also requires that you allow yourself to be vulnerable. If someone challenges how you choose to handle yourself in a particular situation, don't back down. Be confident in your ability to lead authentically and persevere through that person's negativity.

There were many challenging moments throughout Vartika's professional career where she had to work to prove her worth and stand by her own ideas.

I used to have an insecurity because I am from a different background and culture. I thought everybody was looking at me until I came to realize, to a large extent, it's in our heads. That started disappearing when I said, "The person sitting across me has probably similar concerns about their own appearance or experience, in a different way."

Early in my career, while doing a long project, I felt I had to keep repeating what I [was] saying because of my accent. Even if I was making a great point or I had a great idea, it would lose its impact because I was having to explain it in many different ways to get the point across. I think at the end of the day, what I learned is that you don't have to start feeling nervous with that. You have to do your homework (which could be preparation in front of a mirror or practicing with your friends/family) and continue to reiterate the points in different ways. You have to have this conviction that this is a good idea and show your strength through perseverance.

When Vartika was indeed identified as a potential candidate for partnership, she credited it to not only the hard and persistent work but also to those around her that she actively sought the support of.

Being successful oftentimes has to do with being at the right place, at the right time and with the right people. However, those chances do not come if we sit at our desks and wait for them to stop by. We have to actively put ourselves in challenging situations. In one of those moments, success hides.

Being persistent has helped increase confidence, albeit by trial and error. Many times, asking for promotions or advice can get uncomfortable, however I know first-hand that if the person across the desk doesn't know what you want, you have less than 50% chance of getting it.

Strategy 6: Take a Vulnerability Inventory

Vulnerability is the core, the heart, the center, of meaningful human experiences.

—Brené Brown

I am a huge fan of Brené Brown's work. Listening to her on Oprah's *SuperSoul Conversations* podcast was a wake-up call for me, as she tapped directly into some of my personal challenges. I had struggled with an internal tug-of-war between projecting confidence with a "fake it till you make it" mentality and showing my cards about where I felt I truly was in my career and life. What I have learned is that to bring my whole self to work, I have to overcome the fear of embracing vulnerability.

What are the factors influencing your ability and motivation to be more vulnerable at work? Take an inventory. Record your responses to the following questions:

* How was vulnerability viewed in your family? Did you grow up seeing vulnerability modeled? What were the lessons (spoken or unspoken) about being vulnerable? How has this impacted on your vulnerability at work?
* What's your current comfort level with vulnerability?
* What would you do if you were not afraid to be seen?
* What are your top five priorities when it comes to life and work?
* What is your biggest fear when it comes to being your authentic self at work?
* What would be the reward for being authentic at work?
* Women are bombarded with "never enough" messages in the media. Do you use perfectionism as a shield? If so, what scares you the most about putting down the shield and showing your true self?

After you reflect on your response to these questions, go back to Strategy 3. Call a friend with whom you can discuss your answers and explore her own feelings and experiences with vulnerability. How can you reframe your friend's vulnerability as a strength and find a work situation where she can let that strength shine? How can she do the same for you?

Now that you have together identified an area where you want to speak up and shine a light on your strengths, practice out loud with each other. Review your calendar for an upcoming meeting or one-on-one with your boss or another key leader in the organization where you'll have the opportunity to share your unique perspective and to influence how the business operates, how people treat each other, or how decisions are made. Discuss your goals with your friend and rehearse how you can speak up. Ask her to do the same. You can share strategies for preparing your mind-set in advance of those encounters to feel brave enough and empowered to speak from your authentic perspective. If we are vulnerable with ourselves and those around us, we can connect the dots between our unique perspective and its value to our work.

Kate Leiser is head of a new migraine treatment at Lilly. She was hired by Lilly just after graduating from Columbia Business School, when she was pregnant with her oldest daughter. She shared her journey of realizing how she was holding herself back from contributing her voice to then taking those learnings as a leader to help other women find and unleash their voices.

> I will say, it was no easy task. I remember dropping my daughter Maize off when she was three months old at the Lilly day care and walking into the building to start my first day at corporate center. I was like a deer in headlights. I had no sleep. I had just moved to a new city. I'd never worked for a big company. And I was starting a function, marketing, where I technically had no experience. It was a lot. And it took me at least two years—whether that was due to me or the company—to actually feel like I was on solid ground. I think a lot of that was just being a mom and trying to prove myself at the same time.
>
> I was at a stage where I had to prove myself, but I could no longer outwork someone. I just wasn't able to.

> I had to leave the office at 5:55 to go pick up Maize. I
> had to breastfeed. I was juggling my second shift while
> trying to find my way in the first one, my day job.

Kate quickly learned that change was the name of the game and that she could not wait for things to settle to finally be her true self.

> My mind-set had to change. That was important for me
> because I typically take some time to ramp up to a new
> job or a new opportunity. I want to feel confident in
> deeply understanding a subject or situation, and I
> wouldn't speak up until I was solid that I really knew my
> stuff. Then I realized, you can't do that because you'll be
> left behind.
>   People don't know what's going on inside your
> head. They begin to leave you out if you don't speak
> up, and they won't listen to you because you have missed
> half the conservation from not being in the ongoing
> dialogue.

This is valuable advice as you work to ensure you aren't stifling your perspective. You don't have to know everything top to bottom to have something to contribute. Be okay with your vulnerabilities. Waiting for the perfect moment or to become an expert is a trap you need to avoid.

> I realized every time I start a new job, I have no idea
> what I'm doing, but I'm listening and asking simple
> questions that I think are stupid initially, and then I realize
> no one knows the answer. "Comfort is the antithesis of
> progress." That's a line from the movie *The Greatest
> Showman*. Now I tell myself that if I start feeling comfort-
> able, I'm not progressing.

Strategy 7: Help Others Find Their Voice

It's an age-old adage that the best way to truly learn something is to teach it. How can you take your own experiences and wake-up calls and use them to help others show up more authentically?

Learning from her own experience, Kate wanted to make sure that women on her team could thrive and not compromise their values.

> I hired a woman last year on my team in her mid-thirties with two young kids, and her husband was traveling a lot. She brought a decade of experience to the table and decided to move her family to Indianapolis to pursue marketing. At the same time, she had young children. She entered at a level less than where her experience should have led her to be, ultimately, because she didn't project confidence. In one-on-one settings, she was amazing. But as soon as you put her into a larger group, she broke down. By giving her a couple things to help her get grounded and grow, I felt like I knew how to help her.
>
> One: The year she worked for me, she would leave the office at four o'clock every day, and she knew I wanted her to do so. The reason she left the office then was because her younger daughter went to bed at six-thirty, and she wanted at least an hour with her.
>
> Two: Throughout that year, we built her confidence in different settings, encouraging her through trust and my own vulnerability to be true to who she was in front of others. This also allowed her to be more effective.
>
> Ultimately, I promoted her to a new team. And just last week, she was leading our company's global marketing town hall. This is a huge platform and forum, and she was the MC. She hates speaking in public! Yet there she was, and she did amazing. And for me personally, this reinforced the value I bring to this organization and how I can be innovative, disruptive, encouraging, and supportive all at once with myself, the people I lead, and our business. This is now instrumental for my motivation to dig my heels in here at Lilly.

There are two additional very valuable takeaways from Kate's story that I want to highlight:

1. **Find an ally, sponsor, or mentor who has been where you are.** If you are on a tight schedule with a young family or juggling other critical responsibilities that limit your schedule, find an ally, sponsor, or mentor who has been in your shoes. Ideally, you are working for someone who sees the big picture and has your best interests in mind, which means that this person will help you be productive without compromising your priorities. If you can't participate in after-work events that are key to building relationships, find allies who will help you make connections in different ways and keep your brand alive.

2. **Be that sponsor to other women.** We need to help other women find some breathing room as they're moving through life transitions, without stalling their careers and their confidence. We should feel compelled to help them figure out how to grow their networks and increase their visibility and impact while adjusting to a new schedule. Flexibility IS the future of work, and we have to be champions of alternate options for juggling life and work responsibilities. (For more on flexibility and the work + life hacks that will help you thrive, see chapter 7.)

Strategy 8: Do You!

There is no uniform for success, and as long as you are polished, prepared, poised, and presentable, don't be afraid to let your personality shine. Take Susan Axelrod, chief supervisory officer at Merrill Lynch Wealth Management and one of the most well-known and accomplished women in the financial services industry where she held regulatory positions for more than a quarter of a century. I admit that when I read her bio in advance of meeting her, I envisioned a very conservative, tough, no-BS woman. The last thing I expected her to be wearing at our first meeting was a bright pink faux-fur coat. But I soon came to learn that Susan wears a lot of pink as an intentional statement that she will always be true to her personal style and still be taken seriously. Despite the obvious stereotypes and harsh judgment women can face when we project our femininity or even a love of fashion in the workplace, Susan maintains her authenticity. She acknowledges that her wardrobe choices are also a tactic to disarm others, and she finds that people warm up to her because of her approachable style.

> I would say, work hard, be true to yourself, and be bold. Be proud of who you are. My love of fashion includes my love of pink. It's not what you wear. It's who you are when you get in the clothes, and how you treat people, and how you react every day to problems and issues. I'm proud to wear pink and clothes that remind me to bring my full self into every interaction. I had a pink wool hat that I wore, and it was cold in the winter, but I wore it on a video conference call once. And people took pictures, and they thought I was hysterical. That's me. And it does not change my hard-earned results, my tireless work ethic, or my how seriously I take my job.

The Myth of Meritocracy

Many people labor under a misconception of how our economic system works. We have been brought up with the myth of meritocracy: that the system distributes resources—especially wealth and income—according to individuals' merit. Research has found that although merit does indeed affect who ends up with what, the impact of merit on economic outcomes is seriously overestimated.[6] In fact, your relationships and the visibility of your work can overpower or even negate the effects of merit. This creates barriers to mobility and advancement, for women in particular.

Studies show that women more so than men prefer an environment where hard work is rewarded above all else.[7] But in our male-dominated Western business culture, informal networks and being boastful about capabilities and influence are what are critical to advancement. This frustrates women, because they feel that the corporate hierarchy does not reflect meritocratic goals. Millennial women in particular are becoming increasingly disillusioned that their hard work will pay off in equal terms. This causes them to job-hop as the only means they see for increasing pay and responsibility.

Don't underestimate the influential role that relationships and networks play in acquiring the support and feedback you will need to climb the corporate ladder. Although merit is critical, you will need to take the leap and navigate office politics effectively if you are to showcase your capabilities and upward potential. Another leap will be to transform the leadership archetype to reflect more than just the male perspective.

In one interview, I listened to Anne (who wants to remain otherwise anonymous) recount her journey in the airline industry, having been hired from her MBA program. She spent just under a decade working sixty hours a week and moved away from her family to prove her dedication to the company. At first glance, she appeared to be doing well: she had had a title promotion about every two years and was responsible for growing a new department after a key acquisition. She was finally at a point where she believed she had earned a true promotion that would take her to a different part of the company, diversify her experience, and challenge her leadership with broader responsibilities. This was when she received the feedback that blew her mind.

After a talent identification session, her boss told her that the leaders in the room felt that she had a good reputation but that "no one knows what you actually do." This was the wake-up call she needed to recognize that she had not placed enough emphasis on building a network and sharing her key accomplishments. People needed to be more familiar with the impact she was personally driving instead of just seeing her as a loyal and dedicated worker.

For women, lack of flexibility, rigid job structures, and unclear roles and job expectations fuel our desire to just work harder and harder. But putting our heads down and clocking more hours do not work in our favor, especially when the system in which we're working is not designed for us.

Not having access to key relationships beyond your direct day-to-day contacts can lead to a number of other seemingly unconnected consequences: You may make assumptions about the expectations and broader impact of your role, which may limit your understanding of what it takes to advance across the organization and not just within your potentially siloed department. You may also feel pushed to overextend yourself in order to prove yourself worthy. There is always a degree of ambiguity in leadership roles, and there is no perfect standard for how to consistently achieve success. As we continue to deal with double standards and false perceptions of how women lead, we have to avoid the temptation to overcompensate.

These self-limiting behaviors are closely tied to our not having the right flexibility in our jobs to empower us to act on our instincts. We are tied to a strict work schedule, which doesn't adapt to the accelerated 24/7 work and life demands of the modern workforce. Breaking down barriers to achieve greater flexibility can allow us to gain the clarity to effectively manage expectations.

Strategy 9: Unleash Influential Sponsorships

Organizations encourage women in leadership, but often do not address the discrepancy between how women are perceived and how they are recognized in traditional leadership roles—a discrepancy reinforced by traditional performance evaluation and career systems. There are misunderstandings surrounding who has access to personal business networks, largely due to the lack of female mentors and sponsors in senior leadership roles, and men's hesitation to mentor junior women. This is why high-level sponsorship and the ability to leverage key relationships are critical for your advancement to senior-level positions. How can you make yourself and your capabilities known to the influencers you want to bring on your side? For more on connecting with potential sponsors, see chapter 6.

Strategy 10: Bring Men in as Allies

We need to bring men into the Dig Your Heels In conversation to help bust the myth of meritocracy and to gain their support and sponsorship. Learning about the journeys of their female peers and the ways that women may have been held back in their careers due to their gender can be a uniquely transformative experience that builds greater trust.

Here is how asset management firm BlackRock is working to bring in men as allies. Within BlackRock's Women's

Initiative Network (WIN) is a program called Women in Focus. COO Stephanie Epstein was a part of this initiative, in which WIN members met with male managing directors in the largest offices in the United States, and educated them on stereotypes and limiting behaviors, such as asking women to take on "office housework." The program explicitly walked through such examples as note-taking to illustrate how the environment can hold women back from being viewed as full contributors in meetings and as leaders. Stephanie told me,

> We asked our male senior leaders to be really conscious when they conduct meetings if they are constantly asking the same person, a female, to always take notes.
> We asked them to make sure that both genders are sharing these types of responsibilities. It's preeminent, and this is our effort to educate more people. It exists, it's real, and we have to start changing it.

For more on recruiting men as allies, mentors, and sponsors, please see chapter 6.

Strategy 11: Navigate the Politics

Office politics is the use of power and social networking within an organization to achieve changes that benefit certain individuals without regard to the effect on the organization itself. Unfortunately, you can't avoid office politics, and ignoring it can be fatal to your career. Politics is how power is managed on a practical basis every day. From here on out, think of navigating politics as a tactic, not a trade-off. Here are several steps to guide this mental shift in how you outsmart office politics.

* **Evaluate your company's organization chart and the informal network of influence.** Observe and try to understand the relationship dynamics across new teams and at higher leadership levels. Look for the patterns that ultimately lead to consensus or the breakthrough of new ideas. What behaviors are being rewarded?

* **Find your gateway.** What do you see as the blind spots in meeting the needs of the business because politics are getting in the way? Build a case and find allies at your level and above who are stakeholders in the success of your idea.

* **Set a strong example.** Don't participate in spreading gossip and rumors. There is no need to be unprofessional or disrespectful. These behaviors that lack decency will destroy a company culture and cause good people to leave.

* **Develop strong communication skills.** The end game is for your voice to be heard, your ideas to be recognized, and the solutions you put on the table to be implemented—without compromising your values or self-respect. Be ready to make mistakes and get frustrated, but don't take your eye off the end goal. Find allies and reinforce each other's great work.

Good-Girl Thinking

In the corporate sphere, behaving like a "good girl" means taking on roles such as office secretary or office mother when you're actually the one in charge. It's not correcting a client who enters a meeting with your company and addresses the man at the table first when you are actually the boss. It's having to be

* Nice (because girls and women are nice) but not too nice (you don't want to be a pushover)
* Confident (so that you can command respect) but not too confident (or you'll seem like a bitch)
* Forgiving (because women should let things go and not take things so personally)
* Devoted (because women should put their companies above their personal lives)

It is society's perception of how women should behave and our historical lack of permission and skills to counter that perception that prevents us from claiming our authentic feelings and asserting ourselves however we choose. As a mother of two young daughters, I am constantly thinking about this topic.

I hope to raise my daughters with confidence and dignity, but also good manners. I wasn't that sure myself about the fine line between having good manners and being perceived as a "good girl." When is behaving like a good girl a curse, and when is it a compliment? Motherhood and my own internal struggles to be a leader who is both well-liked and respected were my motivations over the past couple of years to learn more about how good-girl thinking affected women at work. I wanted to make connections between what girls learn from a young age and what I was seeing and hearing from working professional women. Part of our struggle is our lack of skills and knowledge to handle conflict with people and to respond to situations that make us uncomfortable. "Good girls" don't argue or act out, after all. At five years old or fifty, we simply aren't given the space or permission to assert ourselves and resolve conflict openly in the way that boys and men do without consequences.

> **Our culture is teaching girls to embrace a version of selfhood that sharply curtails their power and potential. In particular, the pressure to be "Good"—unerringly nice, polite, modest, and selfless—diminishes girls' authenticity and personal authority. The Curse of the Good Girl erects a psychological glass ceiling that begins its destructive sprawl in girlhood and extends across the female life span, stunting the growth of skills and habits essential to becoming a strong woman.**
>
> —*Rachel Simmons,* The Curse of the Good Girl

In an effort to connect with others, women often try to empathize and understand what the other person is going through, with more effort than may be extended in their own direction. Don't get me wrong—empathy is a wonderful strength and serves us well in being authentic and inclusive leaders. But we fall into the good-girl trap when we allow being nice to make excuses for bad behaviors, particularly on behalf of senior leaders. Here's a real-world example (mine).

Right after our acquisition by another company, I was in a group meeting led by a senior vice president. He was demanding that each of us give him a response about each of our team member's career mobility, without offering us time to discuss or providing further background. It was clear that our response could influence team members' future opportunities with the new company, so I refused to answer. This triggered a pretty angry reaction on the SVP's part, and in effect I was called out.

That evening after I put my daughter to bed, I could not turn off my brain. I was suffocating myself, reliving the scenario over and over, trying to find any justification for why this leader approached that conversation with such bullying rhetoric. I was searching for a way to excuse his behavior and to minimize the voice in my head that kept saying, "This is so, so wrong." That's when I landed on some typical good-girl thinking.

I imagined myself in his shoes, trying to grasp at the pressure he was under that had caused him to put all of us on the spot with such paltry information and a lack of background. Why couldn't he begin with a deeper, more transparent discussion? Shouldn't he have walked us through some potential scenarios to assure us that the company valued its people, our teams, each of us? I made the decision to speak to him directly.

I set my alarm for 5 a.m., determined to arrive as early as possible outside his door to show my willingness to be supportive of the tremendous impending changes. In my mind, I believed that if I just could *lean in,* I would show him that I was prepared to act like a leader in this situation. I would also take the opportunity to explain my perspective on how to include each of our team members, their values, and their personal factors in our decisions, and make the case for operating in a transparent, inclusive manner to produce the best path forward for our colleagues and for the company

I knocked on his office door at around 7:15 a.m., and though he certainly looked surprised to see me, he ushered me to a seat in front of his desk. I launched right in:

> I know this must be a challenging and stressful time for you and our leadership team. I do appreciate the enormity of decisions that must be on your mind right now, which is why I wanted to have this conversation in person. I hope you can understand why yesterday's meeting did not sit well with me. The impact to

my team members in the wake of recent news is my top priority, and I just don't believe I have enough information to determine their fate in such an arbitrary way.

I could barely finish my sentence (and I speak very fast!) when he retorted, "Joan, what happened to you? You used to be so ambitious and driven. I don't care about what you think or hope we do to make this situation easier. I want you to focus on your current objectives and execute the results attached to them. And if your team is too distracted by the news to focus right now, then they shouldn't be here."

I was so taken aback by the harshness in his words and tone that my reply was weak: "The only thing different about me today is the lack of sleep in my life with a one-year-old." was all I could muster.

"Oh come on, what are you—one of those parents who doesn't believe in crying it out? Just give your kid some Benadryl and get back in the game here," he said, while essentially dismissing me from his presence.

These moments are sadly and universally experienced by women in every industry. I know this because I've listened to hundreds of stories from women working in global corporations in my quest to better understand their career journey. Sometimes these moments rock us at our core, serving as a clear wake-up call. Other times, we stuff them deep down inside, adding another battle scar as we try to move on.

So let me take this opportunity to offer a "shoulda, coulda, woulda," which is my technique for reviewing a situation in which I have felt powerless and then envisioning the way I could have handled it that would have been a stronger reflection of my values.

The first step (something I work on often) is to turn off that evil inner DJ who loves to spin—in the middle of the night—all the worst tracks of my day and rehash all the awful moments that stress me out. With two children under the age of five, I really need any sleep I can manage, so overthinking at night is not healthy or helpful. I've tried the technique of reminding myself of every situation where I overstressed at night and by morning was much clearer because the situation was never as bad as it seemed in the midnight hour. Therefore in my shoulda, coulda, woulda redo scenario, I would have made a stronger effort to let it go overnight and get some sleep!

Here is how I would reimagine my role in the conversation, even if the SVP still reacted in the same manner:

Me: I know this is a challenging and stressful time for our organization. I do appreciate the enormity of decisions that must be on the table right now, which is why I wanted to have this conversation in person. I value my role as an advocate for my team in this process. Without any details, I am not comfortable determining their fate in an arbitrary way. Can you share anything more about the decisions you need to make to help me get the information you need but also be respectful of my team?

Him: Joan, what happened to you? You used to be so ambitious and driven. I don't care about what you think or hope we do to make this situation easier. I want you to focus on your current objectives and execute the results attached to them. And if your team is too distracted by the news to focus right now, then they shouldn't be here.

Me: *(I stand)* "Okay. I appreciate your time, but clearly we don't share the same approach to this situation. My team is performing beyond expectations, as evidenced in the most recent promotion cycle for them and myself, so I'm happy to give them confidence and encouragement while we move through this transition."

Now, whenever discussions get heated and I can see that the person on the other side is using a command-and-control style, I don't wait around for them to engage in insults. I aim to be clear and strong in my position, then leave with my dignity in hand. It may feel awkward and unresolved, but I'd rather cut out clean than lose face when a respectful outcome is not in the line of sight.

Strategy 12: Pause and Then Engage

One of the hardest maneuvers for women I interviewed was handling themselves in situations where they were challenged by more assertive, masculine leaders, particularly in high-stress meetings like the one I just described. Sometimes they backed down and apologized even though they knew they were in the right. Sometimes their emotions ran so high that they cried, which simply reinforced the damaging stereotype that women are "too "emotional" to be strong leaders. I looked to my friend Heather Jackson, a senior leader at Lilly, for advice on how best to manage conflict and high emotions in the workplace. Her advice? Pause and then engage.

I've known Heather for more than a decade, since our time as sales managers. I've always admired her ability to garner respect from both female and male leaders, who often had very strong personalities. She never seemed to compromise her leadership style and was always herself, regardless of who was around her. I've been most impressed by her poise in stressful situations with some of the most intimidating people; I've never seen her sweat or lose her cool. She doesn't "act like a man" or conform to play the game; she leverages her ability to control her emotions and put time on her side.

> I'd love to always have something really clever to share. But I don't. I listen more than I talk, and I don't argue with people in the moment, even though I might be right. When I see someone react, I don't engage. I don't argue with what they're saying. I try to diffuse the situation with, "You know what? Let me come back to you."
>
> I think maybe that's where some people get themselves in a pickle, because they're trying to argue and do it right on the fly when tension is high and emotions are high. I walk away. I say something to give me some time to pull together what I need to prove my point and get right back in front of that person. I think the other thing is I'm pretty stubborn. I'm not going to ever let anybody see them get to me. In a moment where tensions are high, I'm never going to let them see me rattled.

The following steps sum up Heather's approach to managing conflict in the workplace:

1. **Don't react, and don't back down.** Try not to feed into the other person's emotions even if from your perspective the content of the conversation is unfair or inaccurate.

2. **Diffuse it temporarily.** Give yourself time to get what you need to address the situation. Tell the person, ""You know what? Let me come back to you." But don't run away sheepishly. Walk away with confidence, then quickly get your case together.

3. **Run the scenario by a friend, ally, or mentor.** Before you go in for round 2, get the perspective of a trusted colleague

in the know. Doing so will give you the confidence and insight to make a convincing case once emotions on both sides have cooled down.

This is a heavy chapter because these barriers can be lethal to your career. The good news is that you can navigate them and land on your two feet with your eyes wide open. The success strategies offered in conjunction with all four obstacles (imposter syndrome, stifled authenticity, the myth of meritocracy, and good girl thinking) will help you build good habits so that you can see the pitfalls heading your way and bypass them before they can do damage.

Suppressing our voices and second-guessing our rights are extreme and troubling side effects of sexism in the workplace. I wrote this chapter to help women embrace their own power and voices so that we can build strength in numbers and finally flush out the sexist behaviors in our workplaces. You deserve the career accolades that come your way because of who you are (not what you suppress or who others want you to be) and the relationships you build. You are not "too "emotional," and you're definitely not crazy. You are a woman digging your heels in, and you should be proud. I sure am.

Part 3

MAKING WORK WORTH IT

You will never feel truly satisfied by work until you are satisfied by life.

—Heather Schuck,
The Working Mom Manifesto

Relationships Are Everything

In this chapter, you will learn
* What key relationships every woman must cultivate
* How to build your network before you need it
* How soliciting feedback can strengthen your relationships and advance your career

It's true what they say about its "being lonely at the top." Leadership can be isolating when you need to make tough decisions and deal with unsettling reactions from peers and team members. Facing organizational changes, taking on new challenges, and confronting barriers at work can be intimidating, so much so that you shy away from engaging even when you know you deserve and are capable of more. Preparing yourself mentally for these situations by working through them with your key confidantes and allies will profoundly impact on your courage, confidence, and ability to dig your heels in.

Discovering, developing, and maintaining relationships have been core to the best moments in my life, and I would guess yours as well. We need others to lean on who can relate to our pain, our joy, and even our confusion about what to do next. The times when my relationships have really helped me thrive are during life-stage changes and job transitions. Becoming a parent may be the most obvious life-stage change that impacts on women at work, but caring for aging parents, getting married, or moving in with a partner are also critical times of personal flux when a shoulder to lean on is key. Despite the many resources and networks available online, women still struggle to develop a strong network of friends (both men and women) who have managed similar life and career transitions.

Someone once gave Stephanie Epstein of BlackRock this advice about career transitions: "If you have role, content, and firm, you want to change only one of those at any given time." Well, at one point in her career she changed two, shifting to a marketing role for which she had to learn new content.

> I had to build something completely different, and it was kind of like jumping off a ledge a little bit. You have to put one step in front of the other, but you need a support system to do that. For me, it was the power of my network. I had a bunch of senior women that I tapped into on my own when I joined the marketing team to get good advice about working in a decentralized matrix.

Stephanie's network included women she had known since starting at the firm and colleagues whom she didn't see often but who she knew would be honest with her about her blind spots during this job transition.

> I could ask from their experience, "How do you get all these people together?" and "How do you create a culture of transparency and collaboration?" I got great

insights even if the person was in a different part of the organization, and applied it to marketing.

In an ideal world, we would have the time to shadow, develop new skills, and reflect on personal and professional goals in advance of an official job start date. But often there is only a short window (if any at all) to prepare beforehand, and those first few months are very disorganized and overwhelming. This is why women need to prioritize relationships during these key moves—to help us find our feet in our new roles and provide us the emotional support and air cover needed to maintain our other priorities.

Allies, sponsors, mentors, and coaches are all critical to digging your heels in. You need women and men at all levels of your company to care about you, your career ambitions, and your case for change. You can't do it on your own. I also think it's important to have key confidantes who hold similar responsibilities in their career but work outside your company; talking freely with them about people and problems is easier, as they aren't in the uncomfortable position of working directly with you (or others in your business). In the next section, we'll look at the who's who in your career along with the upside and tripwires of developing those relationships.

Connecting with Key People

There are several core types of relationships that you should invest in. Carve out time to understand their general purpose and evaluate what relationships you feel are lacking in your professional life. The goal of building a network of people who support you and you can support back in return takes time and intention. You must cultivate those relationships so that you can turn to them in situations where you need them.

Many times, in interviews with working women of all ages, they report these questions and statements that intimidate them and leave them feeling overwhelmed.

* Is anyone on my side?
* I don't know what the right thing is to do or who can help me.
* How do I get—and stay—connected with people who can help?
* Forget thriving—I'm still struggling to feel included.

Women face unique challenges in creating networks and building powerful, trusted relationships, largely because established networks and ways of making connections don't cater to them. Did you know that 89 percent of women don't have a sponsor to move them forward in their careers, 68 percent lack mentors, and 61 percent lack role models?[1] In networking, just as in business, it is still, unfortunately, a man's world. This is just one of the reasons why it's so important for all of us to dig our heels in to change the status quo.

Strong relationships with influential advocates are must-haves for securing stretch assignments, receiving clear feedback, claiming your ambition, and advancing to your potential. They're also literally one of the best things in life. The first step is understanding the different types of relationships you need to cultivate.

Role Models

Role models are people who hold values similar to yours and whose personal and professional achievements excite and inspire you. You can learn a great deal from them from afar by emulating their behaviors and actions. But by investing time in building closer relationships, you gain a remarkable source of guidance.

In her former life in the military, associate dean at Tufts University Diane Ryan was very grateful for the few female role models she had during Desert Storm. Diane was in a task force of five thousand people where she was one of only three women. They lived in a giant warehouse complex with just one outdoor area with plywood latrines and a shower designated for the three of them.

> We used to call it walking the gauntlet to where the bathroom was because you'd have to pass through these open bays of dozens of guys sitting out there chilling or playing catch. You could feel the eyes following you as you walked by. The two women that were with me, they were ten or fifteen years older than me and even though I technically outranked them they definitely took me under their wing. They were very seasoned and wise to the ways of the world and they were indispensable in role-modeling how to ignore the stares and project confidence. We called it the "Don't F with Me" attitude. I never felt unsafe because of them. I'm grateful to their example of what amazingly strong, awesome, kick-ass women look like. There are different personal and professional attributes and accomplishments that different people can inspire you with. No one person typically embodies everything you dream for yourself so look around and intentionally learn about the stories of diverse women and men who can inspire your outlook for the future.

Mentors and Mentees

Mentors are people who can guide you and coach you. They are there to answer career questions and offer wisdom on life, too. I recommend seeking out mentors whose personal mission aligns with yours, but who come from different career backgrounds; this offers you a broad range of experience and greater likelihood that your mentors have been exposed to the scenarios you may discuss, which means that they can provide you with more nuanced advice.

Connecting with and mentoring women who are earlier in their careers, as I discussed in the fourth big bold move, is also valuable—and not just for them. You should always have a sounding board in your company who is at an earlier stage than you, someone who can offer a fresh perspective on a situation because they probably have never faced it. Don't underestimate how much reverse mentoring can do for you when you are the more senior professional. You'll be surprised how much your work with mentees can inspire your own actions and help you navigate tough decisions. Mentor relationships are always a two-way street, so be sure to give a heads-up in advance of your meetings about the topics you'd like to cover. If you just want to share a couple of recent work scenarios to ask them for feedback or advice, then drop that in a note too.

Sponsors

Relationships with sponsors create real career traction. These individuals are the ones who can position you for more money and promotions. They are senior leaders in a place to advocate on your behalf and who are willing to put their reputation on the line for you. A key to securing sponsors is demonstrating your value and delivering consistently high-performance results. You have to be visible across your organization and seek out opportunities where more people are exposed to your strengths, your perspective, and your goals. How can you make yourself and your capabilities known so it can attract potential sponsors?

In the very early stages of Susan Axelrod's career when she was a lawyer at the New York Stock Exchange, the backing of a sponsor made all the difference in moving her along her professional trajectory.

> I gave a lot of tours on the trading floor, and one day, the president of the NYSE said to me, "We should have lunch." He wasn't someone that I knew. He had observed me, I guess, bringing a lot of people down to the floor, being proud of the institution, as we all were.
>
> I didn't know what to do. Because what do you do when you're seven levels below the person who says, "Let's have lunch"? I wanted to crawl into a hole. But instead, I went to someone who was a tremendous mentor to me and asked, "What do you think about this?"
>
> He said, "I think you should email him." I said, "Well, I don't even know how to handle it." And he said again, "Just email him." So I emailed him: "You had mentioned to me about potentially getting together for lunch. I just wanted to follow up. I'm available, and I'm happy to work with your assistant."
>
> We had lunch after that, about once a month every year until he retired. And he is now almost eighty years old, and I still see him several times a year at a diner. If I had not followed up on that one comment, I never would've had one of the best professional relationships I've had in my career and life.

Susan's example of sponsorship evolved from being visible in areas at work where she could interact with people of different levels then follow through when an opportunity to build a relationship with someone in an influential position offered to learn more about her. Sponsors can offer you candid feedback on your potential, advice on specific experiences you must pursue to advance, but also must have influence on the decisions that impact on your career. Research has found that women are overmentored and undersponsored and that they also overmentor and undersponsor other women.[2] So you have a dual task here: to earn sponsorship for yourself and also to proactively look for female protégées. In my workshops at numerous corporations, I continue to find that "sponsorship" is a vague and poorly understood concept. In particular, leaders tend not to treat sponsoring people who are different from them as a core competency. Maybe that's why men are 46 percent more likely to have a sponsor than women.[3] This difference adds up over time, as the field narrows and the cumulative effects of sponsorship leading to promotions continue to build.

Women are also more likely to look for sponsors who are also role models, which prevents them from fully connecting with sponsors who are not perfectly aligned with them and utilizing their strength. Finally, women are less likely to utilize the networks and sponsors they do have for self-promotion and advancement, believing that leveraging work relationships is "unbecoming" or "unfair."[4] Believe me, it is not. In larger organizations, you may need one sponsor who is an outsider and two who are insiders, one in your line of reporting and one in a different department or division.

As a sponsor to other women, you must understand the responsibilities in your role that can provide air cover for them and help them take on new challenges and risks to grow their impact. As a partner at PwC who actively sponsors upcoming female and diverse candidates, Vartika Prasad emphasized,

> You need to get deep into the story of a person to both have their back and also to push their limits. You need to understand what motivates them, what are their short-term and long-term goals and be honest in your feedback to them. Most importantly, as a representative of female, diverse, working mom candidates, when you have earned a seat at the decision table, you should effectively use that as a platform to funnel up what you have learned from others and how your organization can help them.

Personal Champions and Allies

These are the people who lift you up when you need an immediate boost—your supporters, people who are committed not only to your success but also to your well-being. They can also be the people with whom you have shared significant experiences, so that even if you don't see each other often, there is enough mutual respect and camaraderie that they always have your back.

Michelle Carnahan of Sanofi says you need two kinds of supporters: emotional and intellectual.

> In the whole emotional supporter piece, for me, for my professional career that has always been James, my husband. "You can do it. Don't let those guys at work get you down. They were wrong and you were right—whether that was the case or not." Nobody has been that more for me than him. Everybody's got to have one of those. It's a total emotional fix. And sometimes there's some intellect with it and sometimes there isn't. But that emotional supporter is that person who can get you back to that place of where you believe you can take on the world.

> And then there are the individuals who I think are the intellectual supporters. These are the people who can validate your work and your impact: "Yes, that was a real contribution you made, and we need to highlight that, and we need to find ways to replicate it in the organization." Or "You know what, no, you may have been in the wrong in playing out that situation." It is important that your intellectual supporters will tell you how it is with facts and feedback—the good and the bad.

One important point that Michelle reinforced about finding these champions is that you have to play that role for someone else first! Anybody who wants that kind of emotional or intellectual support needs to show up similarly for somebody else. Doing so starts a chain reaction, and a champion will come to your side because he or she trusts you to do the same.

Cultivating Key Relationships with Men

As we women are fully aware, the majority of leadership positions are held by men. That is why we need their support, partnership, and sincere commitment to help us advance to positions of equal influence. Bringing men in as allies, mentors, and sponsors is not just a "nice-to-have." It's a necessity.

In my life and career, I have had a number of phenomenal male mentors and found powerful support from male colleagues. New research has found, however, that in the wake of the #MeToo movement, with innumerable instances of sexual misconduct in the workplace finally coming to light, male managers are now three times more likely to say they are uncomfortable mentoring women.[5] So how do we talk to men about being an ally, mentor, sponsor, or champion in our careers and visibly in our companies?

First, we must ensure that safety, comfort, and respect are present in every mentor relationship. You can champion this concept across your organization and help more men become aware of the following straightforward steps they can take to be our allies.

How Men Can Be Respectful Allies, Mentors, and Sponsors to Women without Fear

* **Establish consistent standards and policies across genders.** Men should follow the same policies for meeting with a female mentee as they would for meeting with a male mentee. If a man feels more comfortable meeting with a woman in a public space during work hours, then that is how he should meet with men as well. Having different rules for men and women can end up putting female colleagues at a disadvantage by limiting their opportunities and access to more senior leaders.

* **Educate yourself on communication styles and implicit biases beforehand.** A study found that men are responsible for 70 percent of gender-based interruptions.[6] So, men, please don't interrupt! Keeping this unsupportive action in mind during a meeting can help men avoid certain noninclusive behaviors that perhaps they haven't thought of or realized took place.

* **Establish trust up front.** Ask about the mentee's experiences and listen closely without judgment. You may be totally unaware of the barriers she is facing at work and how the culture perpetuates them.

* **Focus on goals and competencies.** Make sure that professional growth and development is a top priority for

mentor meetings and that the compliments and feedback provided to women focus on professional skills and talents.

* **Be aware of positional bias.** According to Harvard's global online research study, 76 percent of people (both men and women) are gender biased and think of men as more well equipped for a career and women better suited as homemakers.[7] Do you hold certain ideas about which gender is better suited for certain roles on your team? Positional bias may contribute to the lack of women whom men champion and sponsor for leadership positions.

* **Be conscious of reactions and judgments when women speak up.** Women's perceived competency drops by 35 percent and their perceived worth by $15,088 when they are seen as "forceful" or "assertive."[8] Do you react differently or do certain thoughts come to mind when a woman speaks up or disagrees with you, compared to a man? Keep this in mind and speak out if you notice people reacting differently to women than men for similar behavior.

If the men you interact with express hesitation or imply that they feel intimidated in the current climate, suggest reverse mentoring. A reverse mentor is a person, usually in a more junior position, who takes on the role of mentor to a more "experienced" person for the overall purposes of sharing diverse perspectives, mutual learning, and developing skills. Both mentor and mentee benefit. In this case, men would be "reverse-mentored" by women and diverse individuals to understand their experiences at work, the barriers they face, and how men can be stronger allies in the workplace.

Bob Redman is a product director in the Oncology Division at Lilly and a leader in an internal "Men as Allies" initiative. His response to the #MeToo movement and all the stories that have come out of it is to utilize reverse mentoring to become a stronger, more visible ally to the women he works with. He believes that the more we learn about people who may be experiencing a different reality within company walls, the more comfortable we should feel engaging with them. It all comes down to whether you truly care enough about people to get to know them on a deeper level.

The sudden awareness that there are experiences at my company that I have never dealt with, being the most average of white males, really impacted me. Of course, I am not naïve to the injustices that occur outside of these walls, but I definitely was naïve that this happens within these walls. "Not at Lilly—we are all so nice, right?" Even realizing something as simple as the fact that I never have to deal with walking into a room and feeling like I am the only one there who looks like me was a powerful awakening.

Becoming involved in "Men as Allies" first and foremost was a bit selfish; I just wanted to learn more. It grew into wanting to ensure I am always aware and always empathetic to the experiences of my peers and coworkers. As I've become more engaged, I have learned that for true change to take place, everyone needs to be on board, including the "white guys." This personal journey has introduced me to the concept of reverse mentoring, which I have recently put into practice. This is an actionable way to engage with people who do not look like me or come from different backgrounds, with the intent of simply broadening my perspective.

As you seek out male mentors and invest time in building supportive connections, be forthright and acknowledge that you want to ensure that these are mutually beneficial relationships. You can share the advice offered in this section in an effort to be transparent about what would make you feel comfortable, and ask these men how you can offer the same support to them.

Handling Oppositional Relationships

Conflict is always a source of great stress. It can chip away at our confidence in our decisions, block our focus, and, worse, prevent us from being happy at work. There are four rules I've learned about managing conflictual situations with integrity and authenticity (not easy by any stretch, but having some guidelines will help steady yourself to move forward):

1. Approach the person directly and ask for a private discussion. Don't gossip or let the issue fester.
2. Focus on behavior and events, not on personality traits or assumptions about the person's intentions.
3. Listen carefully and keep an open mind to what the other person shares about his or her view of the situation. Acknowledge that you hear the person and that your wish is to improve your working relationship.
4. Know when to involve a third party. If something truly destructive is occurring, you should speak up and address it with the appropriate individuals. Review your company's open-door HR policies to be clear on what to do if a serious line is crossed.

Have you ever faced a situation at work where you felt betrayed by a *female* colleague?

Personally, I have found that conflicts with women have a harsher sting than those with men because I unconsciously place more expectations on my female colleagues and leaders. I've learned in my research that this is a problem I need to overcome and one I want to help you intentionally resolve. We must take each situation at its face without adding emotional details and overthinking the matter at hand.

Gender bias is the most significant culprit in fueling conflict among women. In her book, *What Works for Women at Work*, Joan C. Williams, a distinguished professor of law, mother, and director of the Center for WorkLife Law at the University of California, reviewed hundreds of experimental social psychology studies. She concluded that there are four patterns of gender bias that shape today's workplace challenges: the tightrope, prove-it-again, the maternal wall, and tug of war. For example, the tug of war pattern defines the issue where women receive the message that there is room for only one woman at the top, and that triggers intense competition. I would strongly encourage you to read more about these four patterns and the reference for Joan's book is in the chapter 6 action summary.

In my experiences researching barriers to women's advancement and interviewing many women at different stages of their career about gender bias, here are three common themes and proven strategies for breaking the patterns that pit women against one another:

* **Prove It Again.** This was a pattern that Joan C. William's identified in her work, which I also found to be highly prevalent and derailing within multi-generation dynamics in the workplace. The older women in an organization can appear to apply harsher standards to younger women. These more experienced women may project the feeling that there is only one way to succeed as a woman, because that is what

they had to do, and they have concluded that this is the only way things can be done.

This situation can surface, for example, when, in their pursuit of more flexibility or longer parental leave, millennial women feel unsupported by the more tenured women in their organizations. It's a classically difficult situation because both groups of women feel that their identity and choices are in question.

As a junior professional, do not assume that your more experienced female leaders have it all figured out. After decades of taking on these issues, senior-level women are still navigating tripwires and serious challenges daily, so it's important that you understand why they may have their guard up. Try to separate their support for you from their lack of support for the situation, and know that it is important to help them better understand the impact change will have on you and other women in the organization. We need them (and men) to see the value in evolving the work culture, benefits, and day-to-day practices that are most biased against women. Get your data straight on the situation at hand, with proof points about your perspective and needs as well as the benefits to the company. Set up time to address them directly with the woman leader you perceive as unsupportive of your pursuits. Express your appreciation for her example in changing the role of women at your company, but be firm about how much more you would appreciate her advocacy in achieving a better standard for you and women to come.

* **Queen Bee.** Many women have approached me in frustration when they feel that their work environment is a breeding ground for gender-based competition that feeds

on individual narcissism. Have the courage to break these patterns and approach a woman who you feel is competing with you to come out on top, and deal with her directly. Here is how I would suggest respectfully approaching your colleague: "It is my perception—and I may be wrong— but I think there is some friction in our relationship. I have every intention of being supportive of you, so if I have done something to the contrary or implied otherwise by my actions, please let me know. Can we talk this out?"

* **Gossip Girls.** Gossip can escalate perceptions about women who are champions for the success of all women versus those who appear to want to win solo at all costs. As I mentioned in chapter 5, gossiping lacks decency and can destroy the inclusive company culture you are digging your heels in to build. Don't be quick to judge other women. Aim to respect one another's experiences and decisions and try your best to help them understand your situation and your convictions about what you believe you deserve at work. Encourage other women to work through their conflicts with one another directly. If you hear rumors about a woman or overhear a conversation, you can say, "I wonder if we would dissect a man over behaviors like these." When a friend confides in you about her challenges, try to help her get to the other side with her female colleague or boss without resorting to gossip and derogatory language.

The simple truth is that no woman can change her organization alone. We need each other, and supporting one another is critical to this movement.

Mapping Your Network

What does your network currently look like? List all of the people in your network and categorize them as Sponsor, Mentor, Ally, Role Model, Mentee, or Protégée. If any one category is blank, consider whom you can begin developing a relationship with to fill that hole. If you don't know the person yet, don't let that be a barrier. BlackRock's Stephanie Epstein says that the best approach is to find a way to connect with her or him in person and say, "I am coming to you because I admire your work. I have a lot to learn, and I want to talk to you about what you think it means to be successful here." And, most important, follow up! After your initial meeting, make sure to schedule your next one so that the relationship doesn't languish.

Three Tips for Building Relationships

1. **Take the initiative.** Recognize that 80 percent of the responsibility for growing and maintaining relationships with sponsors and mentors falls to you as the protégée or mentee.

2. **Keep your sponsor or mentor updated.** Let her or him know about your successes and what is going on in your life. Why? Because she or he takes pride in seeing what you accomplish!

3. **Support the members of your network.** Go to their events, like their posts, wish them a happy birthday, send handwritten cards and notes of encouragement. Offer to lend a hand or spread the word about the work or causes they care about.

Exercise: Power Positioning

Power positioning is a conceptual strategy to determine who has the most power and influence in regard to a goal or situation and whom you need to influence.

1. Think about a very specific goal you have for yourself or your team—for example, "I want to evolve my team's effectiveness at annual business planning." Your goal in this exercise is to map out a strategy through charting the people you know and the power and influence they have in relation to this goal.

2. Take a look at your list of sponsors, mentors, allies, role models, mentees, and protégées. Who on your list could have an impact on your goal? You may find that you need to connect with additional people beyond those you originally identified who can influence your goal.

3. For each person, ask yourself:

    • What is her or his position and what connection does she or he have on the outcome or process for achieving my goal?

    • What level of influence do I possess with her or him (low, medium, high), and what level of influence does she or he have on me (low, medium, high)?

    • Can I identify any similar or shared goals between us?

    • Is this person supportive of my leadership vision and ideas as they relate to the specific goal I'm working on?

- What insights from this relationship can I identify that can inform my actions and decisions in an effort to achieve this goal?

4. Take a blank piece of paper and put your name at the center. Illustrate the quality of your relationship with each person by her or his proximity to you at the center of the map. Show that individual's weight of influence on your goal with line thickness. Use arrows to show the main direction of influence. Add a dotted line where connections lie among the people you charted. Place a triangle around your strongest relationships and a circle around those you need to strengthen.

This exercise allows you to evaluate who has the most influence and connection to each step of your journey to achieve your goals. It helps you determine where and how you are spending your time in relation to the goals you have in the short and long terms.

Feedback as Opportunity

You may know that investing in better feedback can have dramatic results. But did you know that soliciting feedback is also a wonderful way to build stronger relationships with the people in your network?

Feedback is an underutilized tool for career management and a conversation tactic that most people actively avoid. There is a fear of hearing something that may disappoint or discourage you, and embarrassment may be the result. This can hold managers back from giving it and from individuals pursuing it. Yet, healthy and productive work relationships are created and strengthened by clear and consistent feedback to help one another grow to achieve their goals. Sadly, there is a feedback gap when it comes to women. Many executives face great challenges giving feedback to female and nonwhite candidates coming up the line. That is because most executives are white males, and although white males are good at talking to and advising other white males, they are often afraid to give candid feedback to women or people of color.

When you actively solicit feedback from the people who can influence your career, it is a signal to them that you respect their opinion and are eager to grow and advance. They will appreciate your vulnerability, admiration, and drive, making them more apt to want to help you, especially if you use those conversations to be specific about the ways you want to grow and improve. What's more, the intimacy and vulnerability of the feedback process will strengthen your unique bond with the person giving you the feedback and make her or him more invested in your success.

Sandra Altine, managing director for diversity and inclusion at Moody's, believes that women's receiving constructive feedback will be one the of the key drivers of change toward equal representation.

> I work with all generations of women (boomers to millennials), and I've learned firsthand what challenges continue to persist in the pursuit of transformation. For women, and women of color in particular, to progress, it's paramount that these barriers be removed. One of the key drivers of this change is ensuring women receive feedback.

According to Sandra, feedback that is clear, specific, and direct and that focuses on an individual's strengths and development areas is what will help with the change we are seeking. Common examples of the unclear feedback she comes across include, "You're doing great—keep doing what you're doing!" "She's not a team player," and the ever-popular "She has sharp elbows." These statements are not helpful: they are not specific and don't point to or define a particular behavior.

Research strongly supports that women are less likely to receive specific feedback tied to outcomes, whereas men receive more specific guidance on what is needed to get them to the next level of seniority in their organization. In fact, only 12 percent of women report being satisfied with the quality of the feedback they receive.[9] Given this sad truth, it is up to you to drive the feedback conversation and use it to your advantage.

Sandra counsels women not to leave a performance review meeting without fully understanding what, if anything, needs to change.

> Ask for clarity, ask questions to understand, and paraphrase in your own words what you are hearing for further clarification. While these approaches might appear simple, it's important to take action during the meeting or have a follow-up meeting to gain more clarity. Your career depends on it! Simply put, getting direct and specific feedback is one of the most important elements for career progression.

Tips for Getting Good Feedback

* **Lead the conversation.** When you proactively ask for feedback, the person you're asking is freed to be more honest, because he or she knows you genuinely want to hear his or her opinion.

* **Be specific about your goals.** When you're specific about what you want feedback on and why, the person you're asking will have a better idea of what you need to improve and how he or she can help you. Tell the person, for example,

"These are the specific two jobs that I want to do next. How do we make that happen?

* **Push for more details.** Don't accept platitudes. Yes, you may be a great employee, but you're not perfect. Ask the person, "What will it take to get me the VP title I'm after?"

Heather Jackson of Lilly thinks controlling the conversation is key to moving up and making the most of feedback.

I've not gotten a ton of constructive feedback unless I dig in and ask for it and not take, "Oh, everything is great." I have found that in my own career conversations with people, I've actually had to drive them. I've had to say, "What is my gap?" If they say, "We don't really see you having a gap," I'm like, "Well, then would you put me in this role?" Then they say, "Well, no." So I have to ask, "Okay, well why?"

Be more direct and forward and ask those questions versus, "Oh, I don't have a gap? Great. This was a great conversation," and walk out the door.

Networking for Women

Have you ever wondered whether it would be worth your time to attend networking events and conferences geared toward women? I want to share some research which confirms that these programs lead to improved financial and intellectual outcomes. The results are outlined in a study led by Shawn Achor, the best-selling author of *The Happiness Advantage*, who has become one of the world's leading experts on the connection between happiness and success.[10] The study followed twenty-six hundred working women across functions and industries who attended the Conference for Women, an event held in several US states, paying close attention to the demographic and psychographic differences between women who elect to attend a conference or not. The control group was composed of women who signed up for a conference but had not yet attended. The study tracked two categories of positive outcomes for the women who attended the conferences: financial rewards and intellectual rewards. Some examples of the findings: In the year after connecting with peers at one of the Conference for Women events, participants' likelihood of receiving a promotion doubled whereas less than 18 percent of the women who'd signed up for the conference but had yet to attend received a promotion; in one year, attendees had tripled the likelihood of a 10+ percent pay increase versus only 5 percent of the women in the control group received a pay increase of more than 10 percent; 78 percent of attendees reported feeling "more optimistic about the future" after attending. A positive mind-set can affect other aspects of life. All of these findings connect to an important takeaway in Shawn's book, *Big Potential,* which outlines his research to prove that the greatest predictor of success and happiness is social connection.

Aside from formal networking conferences, internal communities of women can be powerful in working toward the goal of transforming a company. If you join a women's network or employee resource group, get clear on what your underlying beliefs and attitudes are about advancing and supporting women. How do these fit with the network's goals and areas of focus? Where do you see your company falling short? Do you have any ideas on how to shift the culture? Who can you partner with, mentor, or sponsor to begin changing the game? And, most important, don't look for someone else to tell you where to sign up and how to get involved. Jump in and show other network members what you can contribute to make the biggest impact.

Always Be Connecting

Zoe Baris, marketing manager of Lancôme Makeup at L'Oreal, sees relationships as a web, with every connection leading to something else, directly or indirectly. Each relationship has something to offer, but you don't always know what that will be, and you don't know when you'll find it.

> I admire people for different things, so that I don't expect all I want to be is wrapped up in just one person. For some people, I admire them as a working mom, and others it's for their style of leadership in tough situations. Each connection I make leads me to another person or even to opportunities. I didn't just get on the board of Ronald McDonald House; it happened because I went to a book signing and met this person who really impressed me. I wanted to get to know her better, so I then brought a bag of L'Oreal stuff to have coffee with her. She made the introduction because one of her mentoring advice tips to me was to spend time giving back and serving on a board that needed a fresh perspective. Everything is a web of connections, and I think we all have something to offer one another.

My personal motto is, "Who you know can give you power, but it's how well they know you that can open doors." Relationships take time. Be open and willing to share your life with those around you.

Life + Work Hacks

In this chapter, you will learn
* The types of flexibility to consider and prioritize for your life
* The extreme jobs that lead to burnout and prevent us from digging our heels in
* How to own your time and fully integrate work and life in a sustained way

Baby boomers advocated for work-life separation, generation X pushed for work-life balance, and now millennials are demanding that work and life coexist. Regardless of our age or whether we have a partner, kids, pets, professional hobbies, or any number of other personal responsibilities, we are all struggling to make it work in this messy 24/7 world. Superficial advice tips just don't cut it in this category anymore, and "work-from-home Fridays" are not always the most productive solution.

We all struggle to make life and work *work,* but the barriers facing women are much more pronounced than they are for men—especially if you want to have a family. Did you know that pay parity between the sexes begins to drop the minute a woman chooses to have kids, and it never recovers? Not only does that pay gap widen; so too does the opportunity gap. The perception of working moms as unfocused and less reliable employees is a huge barrier to career advancement. And how often have you heard of companies being reluctant to hire women of childbearing age for fear that they will get pregnant and leave? Even if it was just once, that's too many times.

I once attended a breakfast meeting at the Wing, a women-only coworking space in New York City. Beth Comstock, former chief marketing officer and vice chair of General Electric, was the host, and she asked each woman to share what was on her mind. One millennial woman made a remark that really struck me: "The narrative we hear as young women from more experienced successful women feels false."

She described advice she's listened to at panels inside and outside her company from women who shared their career journeys from the perspective of an opportunity-cost analysis. They focused predominantly on what you should be prepared to sacrifice personally to achieve your professional goals. She knew these women had a world of good intentions to inspire and empower younger women to keep their eyes wide open as they drive their careers. But their message did not land well.

Raised with an entrepreneurial mind-set and constantly bombarded with the pressure to disrupt the status quo, the

next generation of young women are (rightly) refusing to sacrifice. Instead, they want work + life hacks. I define *hack* as a
clever solution to a problem. Millennial women want the gritty
battle stories, and they want every Instagram-worthy detail
of the tricks the women before them have unearthed to bring
about their big lives.

* What do you do to stay present, disconnect, and keep sanity in your personal life while leading an organization of
  hundreds of people?
* How on earth do you stay healthy and fit during the sea-
  sonal cycles when business hours spike?
* How did you figure out how to travel abroad for work while
  nursing a newborn?
* How did you negotiate your biggest salary jump without
  alienating your partner as you started to out-earn him or her?

Women need to know that living a full life inside and outside of work is truly possible—and that we have to fight for
it. We have to dig our heels in to create a workplace that works
for us and all of our priorities. In this chapter, women share
their tripwires and the hacks they learned along the way to
stay healthy and happy and to bring some harmony to the
multi-hyphened demands that make their worlds go round.
But first, a few words on the concept of flexibility.

Flexibility 101

We all need to understand the concept of flexibility and how
to use it to thrive in the office and at home. It is a key negotiation factor for work-life integration. I believe that flexibil-

ity is not a perk of privilege or seniority; it's a benefit that all women should have access to and be armed to negotiate for. Planning, prioritizing, communicating needs, asking for help, outsourcing activities, and valuing self-care time are the consistent best practices of women who feel they have a version of flexibility in their work.

I have learned a great deal about flexibility from my friend Anna Auerbach, cofounder of Werk, a company with technology to put flexibility data and insights into the hands of companies to help them work smarter for women. According to Anna, there are three types of work flexibility:

* When you work (time of day)
* Where you work
* How ad hoc or set that schedule is

Consider your needs and your life outside of work. What kind of flexibility is most important to you? Which type is your company most willing to offer you? If your answer to that second question is "none," you may be working in what's come to be known as an "extreme job."

Extreme jobs are defined as working sixty hours or more per week in a high-paying job with at least five of the following characteristics:[1]

* Unpredictable flow of work
* Fast-paced work under tight deadlines
* Inordinate scope of responsibility that amounts to more than one job
* Work-related events outside regular work hours

* Availability to clients 24/7
* Responsibility for profit and loss
* Responsibility for mentoring and recruiting
* Large amount of travel
* Large number of direct reports
* Physical presence at workplace at least ten hours a day

Across the board, people with extreme jobs report that their work impacts on their ability to craft happy and healthy private lives. About 81 percent of women feel that their extreme job undermines their health, 76 percent feel that their extreme job gets in the way of a strong relationship with children, and 59 percent feel that it gets in the way of a good relationship with their spouse.[2]

Extreme jobs push women out of the workforce. In Anna's research, she found that 69 percent of women said they wouldn't have off-ramped if their companies had offered flexible work options, such as reduced-hour schedules, job sharing, part-time career tracks, or short unpaid sabbaticals.

A Hack-a-thon of Takeaways for Work + Life

The traditional career path (whether extreme or not) tends to be less appealing than a more cyclical path that allows women to define success in more holistic terms of personal fulfillment rather than just power. So how can women attain flexibility without sidetracking their careers? In the next sections, read the practical work + life hacks from women at all levels to find out!

Hack 1: Stay Connected to What Matters

For Michelle Carnahan of Sanofi, the key to successfully integrating life and work is having a good partner.

> You have to have a good partner, whoever that partner is. If it's a neighbor, if it's a husband, if it's a wife, a sister, a brother, a best friend, an assistant, a village, or all of these. Whoever that person is for you, you have to have a partner. You can't do life alone. I'm just convinced of that.

Her second guiding principle is to establish outside-of-work nonnegotiables: your Thursday night CrossFit class, no work talk before 7 a.m., attending your kids' piano recitals—whatever is important to you.

> Then whatever those things are, you have to have some tactics that you practice. One of my tactics was, my kid was not going to be the last kid in day care. Now he may have been the first one there, and I may have missed a few baseball games or may have missed a few field trips, but he was never going to be the consistent last kid at day care! I have no idea why I picked that tactic, but it was a tactic that satisfied me, and it got us dinner together on most nights when I was in town.
> So to me, there is no recipe for doing this; everybody has to do it in their own way. But I do think everybody needs a partner. I do think everybody has to have some things they believe in, and I do think everybody has to have some tactics that they put in that work for them, that they have to follow. And then you have to be agile.

My advice: Identify three nonwork priorities and your tactics for fulfilling them. If it's an evening workout, figure out how to make it clear to the people who may need you at that time that you won't be around then and will get back to them afterwards. If it's no emails on the weekends, draft an automatic email response to assure people that you'll be back on the ball come Monday morning.

Hack 2: Create an Air-Cover Plan

Life doesn't stop just because you're not at home. Who will water your plants? Feed your dog? Look after your kids? Get your mail? And what about at work? To whom can you turn to deal with emergencies while you're away? Creating a network of friends, services, and colleagues to cover you during these times is key, says BlackRock's Stephanie Epstein, who is also a mother of two.

> First of all, I would say sometimes I feel like my life is being held together by a Band-Aid. But other times, it's like a well-built machine. When I'm in New York, my husband, Andrew, a physician, and I coordinate to be home for the kids, each taking two opposite nights to work late. On those two days, I can plan late meetings and do things for me. And that has been the most transformational change I've made when I'm local.
> When I'm not local, it's heavily relying on Andrew, my nanny, and my SWAT team network of other moms in the school! Here is a really great example of why I need them. My oldest is in kindergarten, and there's a lice breakout literally every single week at NYC schools. My SWAT team of moms from school know when I'm traveling, and they go straight to my nanny and tell her about lice during drop-offs and pickups. So that actually gives me a lot of comfort, because I know that my child will be hopefully lice free when I am traveling throughout India.

My advice: Map out whom you can call to help with which personal and professional responsibilities before you need them, so that when the time comes, all you have to do is activate your network.

Hack 3: Maintain Relationships with Nonwork Friends

Ambitious women driving hard toward their career goals in inflexible traditional organizations can find it easy to become hyperfocused "work martyrs." Millennial women in particular are identifying "work martyr" as a badge of honor, not taking all of their fully earned vacation time and expressing more pronounced guilt about burdening others with time away from work.[3] In the short term, this slave to their work obsession may boost their careers, but in the long term, it can only lead to burnout. Making time for friends outside of work is a form of self-care that can counter this hyperfocus on work. Nonwork friendships keep you grounded and remind you of the other parts of your life that may be easy to neglect while putting in hours at the office.

Kristen Shea is a vice president at The Kinetix Group and has been on the fast track in the health care industry ever since her graduation from Georgetown University eleven years ago.

I began my consulting career traveling every week—it sounded like an amazing opportunity at first to learn and grow in many ways in different cities and communities. What I quickly learned was, it then took a lot of effort and self-awareness on my part to maintain and grow my personal relationships while on the road. I am an avid list maker and I have learned that the most important priorities at the top of my list Monday morning are not what I have to get done for my clients for the week, but to touch base with my friends even if it's over text, email, or a quick phone call. We are all at very different places in our lives, but maintaining that communication channel for me has given [us] the opportunity to stay in touch and create the space we may need from our routine, which we are so engrained in. I save one night a week for non-work activities and stick to that—creating boundaries has enabled me to refocus my energy on important relationships that inspire my ideas and creative drive in the work place and outside. One of my most cherished traditions is that a group of my college girlfriends [and I] have a monthly dinner at one of our apartments, and we haven't missed a month in three years. We have all made a conscious effort to be engaged with each other, and it is something we value every time we get together. We all work hard, some have families, we all have less hours than we can count to do things for ourselves, and yet we all recognize and know it is important for our relationships and growth as women to maintain the strong bonds we built as millennials.

As busy as her days are, Stephanie of BlackRock makes sure to put time for hanging out with mom friends in her calendar to remind herself (and her workplace) that it is a nonnegotiable priority.

So a lot of moms do school drop-offs and pickups, and I don't. I can't afford to do that because I need to be at work really early. At first I felt like I was so disconnected and never managed to make plans work out. So I've created a process where my assistant will actually set up a breakfast once a month on a day where she knows I can do drop-off and hang with a mom or group of moms for an hour afterwards at a restaurant near the office. Because my assistant organizes it all, it actually happens consistently. So it's just working it into whatever infrastructure works for you. And it's really important for me to see them, because that is my community that surrounds my children and my family.

My advice: Make time with nonwork friends official by scheduling it into your work and life calendar. I know you may not have someone to whom you can delegate this responsibility, but it's important enough to find some way for it to become a priority. Try using a regular online calendar system and set a reminder on your phone once a month to reach out and make plans. Even the act of setting a reminder will keep it top of mind.

Hack 4: Optimize Your Off Time

If early Friday dinners with your family are a priority, consider when you can make up that time elsewhere. Jen Schubach of Pfizer likes to work late some nights and early others so that her Fridays always end early. Here's her hack for making the transition from weekend to weekday easier:

> I'll send a bunch of emails on a Sunday night after the kids are in bed, but I'll delay the delivery until Monday so that people who work for me aren't freaking out but my Monday becomes easier.

My advice: Find the dead time in your schedule and use it efficiently to allow more space for your priorities.

Hack 5: Keep Your Skills Fresh

Working at larger institutions can be challenging, and the glacial pace at which change often occurs can make you crave a more fast-paced start-up environment. Before you jump ship, consider how you can stay with your company to leverage all the equity you've already built while keeping your mind and skills sharp for your continued climb up the ladder. Kate Leiser of Lilly has this tip for staying energized in her corporate career:

> I like to start things and then pass them along. I think right now with this job in many ways I'm giving myself freedom, and my leadership is giving us freedom to act like a start-up, even though we have all our processes in place. I'm figuring out how to thrive in this big thirty-six-thousand-person company where the habits of agility and looking for inspiration outside of our industry weren't always appreciated or known. I'm satisfying my hunger for that start-up experience by continuing to build knowledge, relationships, and skills that will make me more

successful. If I wasn't learning anything, I would jump ship, but I continue to learn a ton. And I want to be here and prove that we can be nimble, innovative, and transformative, particularly for women.

My advice: Even if you've been at your company for years, channel your inner entrepreneur to champion a new initiative. It may or may not be related to your current role, but make sure it aligns with your long-term goals. The energy boost from working on something new and growing new skills will only add to your success.

Hack 6: Pace Yourself during Transitions

Things are slow . . . until they're not. Managing life and work priorities may be the most difficult during times of transition—for example, when relocating your family for a new job. There is a world of innovation that is overdue in the area of corporate relocation. Despite the many pamphlets, moving company guides, and "Welcome to Your New City" websites, this can be an overwhelming experience, stalling your ability to be effective in your new role because personal demands are in limbo. Prioritizing your needs and those of your family is crucial during these times, and you will need the support of your company as well as your network.

Chelsea Mohler, manager in Lilly's Manufacturing Division, took a promotion that would move her husband and three kids from Indianapolis, Indiana, to San Juan, Puerto Rico. Here is what she learned:

* Research all the relocation resources your company provides and take advantage of them all.

* Anticipate what the new day-to-day routine may be like and talk it through with your family and your new boss and colleagues so that everyone is on the same page.
* Talk with your family about what the next few months may hold (e.g., travel, long days, different housing or child-care situations) to get them comfortable with all the changes.
* Contact someone within your company who is currently in that location—would he or she be willing to help ramp up your relocation readiness?

Chelsea packed up her home and shipped it all to Puerto Rico. Three weeks later, Hurricane Maria hit and devastated the area. You can't always plan for life. Life happens, and this is the time when you need to know that you and your family are surrounded by a support network of people who genuinely care, helping you navigate unforeseen and stressful situations. Inspired by her own experiences, Chelsea created a program at Lilly for women across her company who are moving through key career transitions, such as global assignments and first-time managers to help them feel supported, knowledgeable, and confident so that they can succeed at work and at home.

My advice: In times of change and uncertainty, communication is key. Once you have your work and life priorities clear, make sure that the people who matter are aware so that they can support you in your efforts.

Owning Your Time

Even with all the work + life hacks out there, it is not always going to be smooth sailing as an ambitious woman who also has life priorities. Sometimes it's the worst of both worlds, Jen Schubach admits.

It's not so easy. It's really hard. I'm not saying that it isn't also hard to stay home, but it's not all "You go girl, everything is great!" and you walk out the door with this briefcase where you go to work and your kids are smiling. No, it's super hard sometimes because one kid is crying HARD. Or you know your child care just isn't going to handle something the way you would if you were there personally.

At other times it's the best because you get to fulfill all the different parts of you and really thrive as a person—not just as an executive or a mom or a partner or a daughter. And when you assume agency in regard to your time, goals, and priorities, you can work to your highest effectiveness over a sustained period.

What are your top five priorities in your personal life? What are your top five priorities in your work life? What boundaries do you need to establish to accomplish both sets of priorities?

Conclusion

Be What She Sees

Regardless of your position or life circumstances, you deserve to work in a place that values you as a whole person, not one in which you have to hide the parts of you that don't fit into the corporate mold developed over a hundred years ago by men with totally different priorities for work and life. Sure, you can jump ship to a new company that *seems* as though it values you more and where you *think* you won't have to face the same barriers to advancement . . . maybe. But you never really know what you're getting yourself into until you're in it. And what about all the equity and institutional knowledge you left on the table at your old company? You'll have to start from scratch developing your reputation and political savvy to start making your way up the ladder again.

Or . . . you can dig your heels in to create change where you are, with all you know—people and processes—and make a real difference in your life and in the lives of all the women who come after you.

Digging your heels in is about moving toward solutions—for yourself and your career, for your business, and for the world. It is a unique way to leverage the blood, sweat, and tears you have put into your career at your company and create the roles and the workplace that you deserve. And it is truly the only way we, collectively, will begin to create change in the world of business so that all women can thrive.

Digging your heels in is how we will eventually achieve equal value—with you as one of the trailblazers making it happen! The pride and fulfillment of being a change maker are not to be taken lightly. Your story of dealing with gender bias and of overcoming situations that held you back from being your authentic self will become a model for others, planting the seeds of transformation far and wide. Representation matters. You can be what women of all ages and backgrounds see and you never know who is watching that needs the inspiration that only your story can ignite.

In January 2000, I came back to the University of Pittsburgh following winter break with a new responsibility: student government president, representing a student body of more than eighteen thousand undergraduates. I had always been a leadership book junkie and over the break had clocked countless hours at Barnes and Noble. Finally, back on campus, one of my mentors handed me a book, *Hesselbein on Leadership* by Frances Hesselbein, CEO of the Girl Scouts of the USA. This was the first leadership book I had ever seen that had a woman's face on the front cover and was about her own leadership principles.

Frances tripled minority membership in the Girls Scouts during her tenure, published the first marketing materials in Spanish, increased the curriculum to cover social issues such as drug use and teen pregnancy, and invested in her leadership team through a professional training program designed by the Harvard Business School. In 1998, she was awarded the Presidential Medal of Freedom, the nation's highest civilian honor, presented by President Bill Clinton, who called her "a pioneer for women, volunteerism, diversity, and opportunity." President George H.W. Bush also appointed her to two commissions on national and community service. Being exposed to Frances at a pivotal moment in my early leadership experiences was transformative and has impacted on every goal and dream I've had since. And she continues to inspire my own daughters and their friends. Believing in Frances and seeing strong women like her champion the absolute rights and values of women in the workplace and community strengthened my belief in me! By seeing Frances in action, I knew I had what it takes to be a leader. Leadership is not about a title. Anyone at any age and with any job or role can embody inclusive leadership and have a positive impact on those around them.

Women embody unique attributes as leaders, attributes that every organization needs. You are that leader, and you always have been. Now it's time to dig your heels in and show the world what you can do.

The Business Case for Change

What's in It for Your Company

> **Businesses cannot thrive when half of the talent pool is ignored.**

Gender-diverse organizations outperform organizations with a weak diversity and inclusion climate across the board:[1]

* Four times higher in demonstrating innovative behaviors
* Three times more employee confidence in the performance of their organizations
* Two times more customer focus
* Three times higher employee engagement levels
* Fifty percent less intention to leave the organization in the next twelve months
* Two times more likely for employees to collaborate with others
* Four times more training and development to do the job effectively

Why? Reputation, Revenue, Productivity, and Retention

＊ **Reputation.** People want to work for companies that value gender diversity and make it a priority because when prospective employees see women in leadership, they recognize opportunities for progression.[2]

＊ **Revenue.** McKinsey reports that advancing women's equality could add $12 trillion to global growth by 2025.[3] What is more, the research shows that companies with three or more women on the board outperform companies with all-male boards by 60 percent on return on investment, 60 percent on return on equity, and 84 percent on return on sales. In other words, a move from no women board members to 30 percent representation is associated with a 15 percent jump in profit![4]

＊ **Productivity.** Women improve the quality of decision-making because[5]

- Men and women have different viewpoints, ideas, and market insights. Access to both enables better problem-solving, ultimately leading to superior performance at the business-unit level.

- A gender-diverse workforce provides easier access to resources, such as various sources of credit, multiple sources of information, and wider industry knowledge.

- A gender-diverse workforce allows the company to serve an increasingly diverse customer base.

＊ **Retention.** Inclusive cultures have 22 percent lower turnover rates due to increased morale, opportunity, and equality. People perform best when they feel valued, empowered, and respected by their peers. Neurological research shows that we experience our most productive, innovative, and collaborative times at work when we feel that we are a part of the team, which is an outcome of an inclusive work-force.[6]

Chapter Action Summaries

This section is your cheat sheet for what you need to do to begin digging your heels in and thriving in your company.

Chapter 1: The Case for Digging Your Heels In (Everybody Wins)

✻ Think about what representation means to you. How would it have changed your career path to be exposed to more women in leadership positions in your earlier years?

✻ Reflect on the skills, institutional knowledge, and relationships you can leverage to begin planting the seeds of change in your company.

✻ Consider the benefits of digging your heels in and building the company you deserve right where you are:
  - To your career
  - To your company
  - To your community

Resources

* www.joankuhl.com
* www.pharmavoice.com/pdfs/2014/pv-1014/HBALeader
  shipPublication.pdf?tracker_id=1538430302#page=18
* www.pewresearch.org/fact-tank/2017/12/14/gender-dis
  crimination-comes-in-many-forms-for-todays-working
  -women/
* http://fortune.com/2017/06/07/fortune-500-women-ceos/
* http://fortune.com/2018/05/21/women-fortune-500-2018/
* http://fortune.com/2018/05/22/fortune-500-companies
  -women-boards/
* www.catalyst.org/knowledge/statistical-overview-women
  -workforce
* www.catalyst.org/system/files/The_Bottom_Line_Corpo
  rate_Performance_and_Womens_Representation_on_Bo
  ards.pdf
* www.mckinsey.com/featured-insights/employment-and
  -growth/how-advancing-womens-equality-can-add-12-tril
  lion-to-global-growth
* www.pwc.com/sg/en/diversity/assets/female-millennial-a
  -new-era-of-talent.pdf.
* www.vitalsmarts.no/uploads/9/4/6/7/9467257/women-in
  -the-workplace-ebook.pdf.

Chapter 2: Making the Decision

* Diagnose your company culture to get clear on its current
  and future ability to empower women in an equitable, inclusive environment.
* Respond to the DYHI Reflection Questions to help you
  make this very personal decision.

* Before you make a move, take some time to acknowledge the emotions and thoughts that come up from your decision. Then evaluate the situation and your next moves before rushing into anything. Trust your capacity to reflect and listen closely to your thoughts.
* Be confident in your ability to use your natural judgment and critical thinking skills—you've got this!

Resources
* www.pnas.org/content/114/18/4637
* https://leanin.org/circles

Chapter 3: Setting the Stage for Success

* Get clear on your unique career vision. You can start by thinking about the people inside and outside your company who inspire you.
* Take the initiative by filling in the gaps at your company that only you can fill.
* Begin to create your future with these seven steps:
  1. Take a personal inventory
  2. Map your goals
  3. Reimagine your company
  4. Identify resources
  5. Invest in content and connections
  6. Seek out other women to learn about their vision
  7. Make the case for your company (use the stats in The Business Case for Change section as a start!)
* Be vulnerable with your vision and compassionate toward yourself along the way. You are enough.

Resources

* The Business Case for Change section of this book
* Events and organizations to explore:
  * Alt Summit (www.altitudesummit.com/)
  * Black Career Women's Network (https://bcwnet work.com/careeressentials/)
  * C2: ColorComm (www.colorcommnetwork.com/)
  * Create + Cultivate (www.createcultivate.com/)
  * Diversity Inc. (www.diversityinc.com/)
  * Ellevate Network (www.ellevatenetwork.com/)
  * Summit 21 (https://21ninety.com/summit21/)
  * Forbes (www.forbes.com/forbes-live/)
  * Fortune: The Most Powerful Women & Most Powerful Women Next Gen (www.fortuneconfer ences.com/fortune-mpw-next-gen-2018/)
  * GirlBoss Rally (www.girlbossrally.com)
  * Grace Hopper Celebration of Women in Computing (https://ghc.anitab.org/)
  * HBA (www.hbanet.org/)
  * ICAN's annual Women's Leadership Conference (http://icanglobal.net/our-events/conference/)
  * Influence Network (http://theinfluencenetwork.com/)
  * Makers (www.makers.com/conference)
  * Massachusetts Conference for Women (www .maconferenceforwomen.org/)
  * National Coalition of 100 Black Women, Inc. (www.ncbw.org/)
  * National Congress of Black Women (https://ncb winclac.org/)
  * Pennsylvania Conference for Women (www.paco nferenceforwomen.org/)

- Powerful Women's Weekend (www.thepowerful women.org/)
- Propel Women (www.propelwomen.org/)
- S.H.E. Summit (https://shesummit.com/)
- SXSW (www.sxsw.com/)
- TED Women (www.ted.com/attend/conferences /special-events/tedwomen)
- Texas Conference for Women (www.txconference forwomen.org/)
- WIN Summit (http://winsummit.com/)
- Women in the World (https://womenintheworld .com/)
- Women of Color Leadership and Empowerment Conference (WOC) (https://colormagazine.com /women-of-color-2018/)
- Yellow Conference (https://yellowco.co/)

Chapter 4: Big Bold Moves

* Keep each of the following eight big bold moves in mind, identifying which action is appropriate to take when, within the context of your life and professional situation. But, do something.

1. **Model inclusive leadership:** Show them how inclusive behaviors deliver better results for everyone.
2. **Take control of your growth and development:** Map out the developmental opportunities you want to pursue and proactively discuss them with your direct leaders.
3. **Engage your employee women's network:** Use it as a tool to increase the talent pipeline of women, and foster relationships and a stronger sense of belonging and community.

4. **Lift as you climb:** Pay it forward by mentoring younger women.

5. **Ignite an industry-wide conversation:** The conversation about achieving gender parity and building a more inclusive workplace culture is one that everyone in your organization (and industry) needs to be having.

6. **Get to equal representation:** Start with your own team and get specific on your goals for achieving 50-50 representation of women.

7. **Get pay straight:** Do the homework. Initiate salary discussions with your supervisor. Continue to review your pay and remain aware of market comparators.

8. **Advocate behind closed doors:** Get in the room where talent decisions are made.

Resources

* www.jpmorganchase.com/corporate/About-JPMC/women-on-the-move.htm
* www.ey.com/gl/en/issues/business-environment/women-fast-forward
* www.ceoaction.com/about/
* www.gartner.com/ngw/eventassets/en/conferences/chrus18/documents/human-resource-us-key-takeaways-2017.pdf
* www.bentley.edu
* https://hbr.org/2018/02/dowomens-networking-events-move-the-needle-on-equality#comment-section
* https://womenintheworkplace.com/Women_in_the_Workplace_2016.pdf
* www.rachelsimmons.com/books-and-advice/articles-and-girltips/
* https://katetparker.com

* www.jessicabennett.com
* www.hollywoodreporter.com/rambling-reporter/shonda
  -rhimes-talks-netflix-pay-at-elle-women-hollywood-awards
  -1152606
* www.mckinsey.com/industries/media-and-entertainment
  /our-insights/we-are-wrong-about-millennial-sports-fans
* Nonprofits that focus on female empowerment to pursue
  volunteer opportunities
    • Girls Hope of Pittsburgh (www.girlshope.org/)
    • Girl Scouts of the USA (www.girlscouts.org/)
    • Step Up for Women (www.suwn.org/)
    • Girls Inc. (https://girlsinc.org/)
    • Girls Inc. of NYC (www.girlsincnyc.org)
    • Girls Leadership (https://girlsleadership.org)
    • Girls on the Run NYC (http://gotrnyc.org)

Chapter 5: Overcoming Obstacles

* Gain an understanding of the following self-limiting behaviors that hold women back:
    • Imposter syndrome
    • Stifled authenticity
    • The myth of meritocracy
    • Good-girl thinking
* Use the following strategies to overcome them:
  1. Own your success
  2. Reframe the negative
  3. Call a friend
  4. Cultivate your personal brand
  5. Speak up
  6. Take a vulnerability inventory
  7. Help others find their voice

8. Do you!
9. Unleash influential sponsors
10. Bring men in as allies
11. Navigate the politics
12. Pause and then engage

Resources

* https://diversity.ucsf.edu/resources/unconscious-bias
* www.tci-thaijo.org/index.php/IJBS/article/view/521
* http://psycnet.apa.org/record/2006-01509-016
* https://rowman.com/ISBN/9781538103418/The-Merito
  ' cracy-Myth-Fourth-Edition
* http://time.com/3666135/sheryl-sandberg-talking-while
  -female-manterruptions/
* www.nytimes.com/by/jessica-bennett?module=inline

Chapter 6: Relationships Are Everything

* List all of the people in your network and categorize them as Sponsor, Mentor, Ally, Role Model, Mentee, and Protégée.
* If any one category is blank, consider whom you can begin developing a relationship with to fill that hole.
* Establish and grow relationships with influential people by supporting them as much as you want them to support you.
* Use the Power Positioning exercise to evaluate where and how you are spending your time in relation to your goals.
* Seek constructive feedback from the members of your network to increase their investment in your success.

Resources

* https://hbr.org/2010/05/when-female-networks-arent-eno
* www.forbes.com/sites/bonniemarcus/2015/04/06/why
  -having-a-sponsor-is-important-for-women-and-how-to
  -get-one/#9ba11c745fec
* www.vitalsmarts.no/uploads/9/4/6/7/9467257/women-in
  -the-workplace-ebook.pdf
* www.forbes.com/sites/break-the-future/2016/12/20/think
  -youre-not-biased-against-women-at-work-read-this
  /#32ad57fd7e5a
* www.pwc.com/sg/en/diversity/assets/female-millennial-a
  -new-era-of-talent.pdf

Chapter 7: Life + Work Hacks

* Determine the types of flexibility you want to prioritize for your life.
* Use the following work + life hacks to increase your flexibility without sidetracking your career:
  1. Identify three nonnegotiable nonwork priorities and your tactics for fulfilling them.
  2. Map out whom you can call to help with which personal and professional responsibilities before you need them.
  3. Make time with nonwork friends official by scheduling it in your work and life calendars.
  4. Find the dead time in your schedule and use it efficiently to allow more space for your priorities.
  5. Channel your inner entrepreneur to champion a new initiative that aligns with your long-term goals.
  6. Once you have your work and life priorities clear, make sure the people who matter are aware of them so that they can support you.

* Know that life as an ambitious woman who also has non-work priorities is not easy, but when you assume agency in regard to your time, goals, and priorities you can work to your highest effectiveness over a much longer term.

Resources

* https://www.the-wing.com
* https://www.theriveter.co
* https://hbr.org/2006/12/extreme-jobs-the-dangerous-allure-of-the-70-hour-workweek
* www.washingtonpost.com/news/on-leadership/wp/2017/05/25/millennial-women-arent-taking-the-vacations-theyve-earned/?noredirect=on&utm_term=.ca732d7c27c5

Conclusion: Be What She Sees

* Know that you deserve to work in a place that values you as a whole person, not one in which you have to hide the parts of you that don't fit into a male corporate mold.
* Leverage the blood, sweat, and tears you have already put into your career at your company to create the roles and the workplace that you deserve. It will inspire others.
* Let your story of dealing with gender bias become a model for others, planting the seeds of transformation far and wide.

Notes

Introduction

1. Jay Bazzinotti, "What Should You Do When You Realize You're Underpaid?" *Fortune* (October 4, 2014), http://fortune.com/2014/10/14 /what-should-you-do-when-you-realize-youre-underpaid.

2. Catalyst, *Revealing the Real Millennials: Workplace Gender Bias* (New York: Catalyst, October 6, 2015).

3. Nielsen, "Want More, Be More: When It Comes to Gender Equality, Millennial Women Are More Optimistic about Closing the Gap" (March 8, 2017), www.nielsen.com/us/en/insights/news/2017/when -it-comes-to-gender-equality-millennial-women-are-more-optimistic-on -closing-the-pay-gap.print.html.

4. Kim Parker and Cary Funk, "42% of US Working Women Have Faced Gender Discrimination on the Job," Pew Research Center (December 14, 2017), www.pewresearch.org/fact-tank/2017/12/14/gender -discrimination-comes-in-many-forms-for-todays-working-women.

5. Joy Fitzgerald, "How Lilly Is Getting More Women into Leadership Positions," *Harvard Business Review* (October 23, 2018), https://hbr.org /2018/10/how-lilly-is-getting-more-women-into-leadership-positions.

6. "Women Won't Have Equality for 100 Years—World Economic Forum," *BBC* (November 2, 2017), www.bbc.com/news/world-41844875.

Chapter 1

1. Muhtar Kent, "The Purchasing Power of Women: Statistics," The Coca-Cola Company (October 2010), https://girlpowermarketing.com /statistics-purchasing-power-women.

2. Ibid.

3. Carolyn Buck Luce, "Power of the Purse," *HBAdvantage* (Fall 2014), www.pharmavoice.com/pdfs/2014/pv-1014/HBALeadershipPublication .pdf?tracker_id=1538430302#page=18.

4. "These Are the Women CEOs Leading Fortune 500 Companies," *Fortune* (June 7, 2017), http://fortune.com/2017/06/07/fortune-500 -women-ceos/.

5. Valentina Zarya, "The Share of Female CEOs in the Fortune 500 Dropped by 25% in 2018," *Fortune* (May 21, 2018), http://fortune.com /2018/05/21/women-fortune-500–2018/.

6. Catalyst, *Statistical Overview of Women in the Workplace* (August 11, 2017), www.catalyst.org/knowledge/statistical-overview-women -workforce.

7. Claire Zillman, "These Are the 12 Fortune 500 Companies with Zero Women on Their Boards," *Fortune* (May 22, 2018), http://fortune .com/2018/05/22/fortune-500-companies-women-boards/.

8. Catalyst, *The Bottom Line: Corporate Performance and Women's Representation on Boards* (2007), www.catalyst.org/system/files/The _Bottom_Line_Corporate_Performance_and_Womens_Representation _on_Boards.pdf.

9. Jonathan Woetzel, Anu Madgavkar, Kweilin Ellingrud, Eric Labaye, Sandrine Devillard, Eric Kutcher, James Manyika, Richard Dobbs, and Mekala Krishnan, "How Advancing Women's Equality Can Add $12 Trillion to Global Growth," McKinsey & Company (September 2015), www.mckinsey.com/featured-insights/employment-and-growth/how -advancing-womens-equality-can-add-12-trillion-to-global-growth.

10. Olaiya E.Aina and Petronella A. Cameron. "Why Does Gender Matter? Counteracting Stereotypes with Young Children" (2011), www .southernearlychildhood.org/upload/pdf/Why_Does_Gender_Matter _Counteracting_Stereotypes_With_Young_Children_Olaiya_E_Aina _and_Petronella_A_Cameron.pdf.

11. Joan Snyder Kuhl and Jennifer Zephirin, *Misunderstood Millennial Talent* (Los Angeles: Rare Bird Books, 2016), https://hbr.org/2016/08 /research-millennials-cant-afford-to-job-hop.

Chapter 2

1. Wei James Chen and Ian Krajbich, "Computational Modeling of Epiphany Learning," *PNAS* 114, no. 18 (May 2, 2017): 4637–4642, www .pnas.org/content/114/18/4637.

2. Lean In Circles were introduced and are supported by Sheryl Sandberg, author of *Lean In*. You can learn more about Lean In Circles at https://leanin.org/circles.

3. Kathy Caprino, "How Decision-Making Is Different between Men and Women and Why It Matters in Business," *Forbes* (May 12, 2016), www.forbes.com/sites/kathycaprino/2016/05/12/how-decision-making-is -different-between-men-and-women-and-why-it-matters-in-business/.

4. Therese Huston, *How Women Decide: Whats True, Whats Not, and What Strategies Spark the Best Choice* (New York: Mariner Books, 2017).

Chapter 3

1. Rebecca B. Silver, Jeffrey R. Measelle, Jeffrey M. Armstrong, and Marilyn J. Essex, "The Impact of Parents, Child Care Providers, Teachers, and Peers on Early Externalizing Trajectories," *Journal of School Psychology* 48, no. 6 (2010).

Chapter 4

1. Rita Gunther McGrath, "How a Leader Can Build Psychological Safety," *Wall Street Journal* (May 16, 2017), https://blogs.wsj.com/experts /2017/05/16/how-a-leader-can-build-psychological-safety/.

2. Juliet Bourke and Bernadette Dillon, "The Six Signature Traits of Inclusive Leadership," Deloitte (April 4, 2016), www2.deloitte.com/insights /us/en/topics/talent/six-signature-traits-of-inclusive-leadership.html.

3. Peter F. Drucker, Frances Hesselbein, and Joan Snyder Kuhl, *Peter Drucker's Five Most Important Questions: Enduring Wisdom for Young Leaders* (Hoboken, NJ: Wiley, 2015).

4. Center for Women and Business at Bentley University, "Taking Employee Resource Groups to the Next Level" (Fall 2016), www.bentley.edu/files/2017/03/17/Bentley%20CWB%20ERG%20Research%20Report%20Fall%202016.pdf.

5. Selena Rezvani and Jo Miller, "6 Trends Driving Cutting-Edge Corporate Women's Networks," HR.com (March 3, 2018).

6. Dan Singer, "We Are Wrong about Millennial Sports Fans," McKinsey & Company (October 2017), www.mckinsey.com/industries/media-and-entertainment/our-insights/we-are-wrong-about-millennial-sports-fans.

7. Bertrand Marianne, Goldin Claudia, and Katz Lawrence, "Dynamics of the Gender Gap for Young Professionals in the Financial and Corporate Sectors," *American Economic Journal: Applied Economics* 2, no. 3 (2010): 228–255.

8. McKinsey & Company and Lean In, *Women in the Workplace 2017,* https://womenintheworkplace.com.

Chapter 5

1. "Unconscious Bias," University of California, San Francisco, Office of Diversity and Outreach (n.d.), https://diversity.ucsf.edu/resources/unconscious-bias.

2. Jaruwan Sakulku, "The Impostor Phenomenon," *Journal of Behavioral Science* 6, no. 1 (2011): 75–97, www.tci-thaijo.org/index.php/IJBS/article/view/521.

3. Joseph R. Ferrari and Ted Thompson, "Impostor Fears: Links with Self-Presentational Concerns and Self-Handicapping Behaviours," *Personality and Individual Differences* 40, no. 2 (2006): 341–352, http://psycnet.apa.org/record/2006–01509–016.

4. Jessica Bennett, Saskia Wariner, and Hilary Fitzgerald Campbell. *Feminist Fight Club: An Office Survival Manual (for a Sexist Workplace)* (New York: Harper Wave, 2017).

5. Ian Altman, "Don't Waste Time Fixing Your Weaknesses," *Forbes* (September 21, 2015), www.forbes.com/sites/ianaltman/2015/09/15/dont -waste-time-fixing-your-weaknesses/#3418420a300e.

6. Stephen J. McNamee and Robert K. Miller Jr., "The Meritocracy Myth," *Sociation Today* (2004), www.ncsociology.org/sociationtoday/v21 /merit.htm.

7. Judy B. Rosener, "Ways Women Lead," *Harvard Business Review* (August 1, 2014), https://hbr.org/1990/11/ways-women-lead.

Chapter 6

1. Sylvia Ann Hewlett and DeAnne Aguirre, "When Female Networks Aren't Enough," *Harvard Business Review* (May 2010), https://hbr.org/2010 /05/when-female-networks-arent-eno.

2. Herminia Ibarra, Nancy M. Carter, and Christine Silva, "Why Men Still Get More Promotions Than Women," *Harvard Business Review* (September 2010), https://hbr.org/2010/09/why-men-still-get-more -promotions-than-women?referral=00134.

3. Bonnie Marcus, "Why Having a Sponsor Is Important for Women and How to Get One," *Forbes* (April 6, 2015), www.forbes.com/sites /bonniemarcus/2015/04/06/why-having-a-sponsor-is-important-for-women -and-how-to-get-one/#9ba11c745fec.

4. Ibid.

5. LeanIn.org Study 2018 using SurveyMonkey online poll conducted January 23–25, 2018, among a national sample of 2,950 employed adults. The modeled error estimate is +/-2.5 percent among employed adults; https://leanin.org/sexual-harassment-backlash-survey-results#endnote1.

6. Rolereboot, "In Mixed Gender Groups, Can You Guess Who Talks the Most?" *Role Reboot* (October 22, 2015), www.rolereboot.org/culture -and-politics/details/2015–10-in-mixed-gender-groups-can-you-guess-who -talks-the-most/.

7. Tiffany Pham, "Think You're Not Biased against Women at Work? Read This," *Forbes* (December 20, 2016), www.forbes.com/sites/break-the -future/2016/12/20/think-youre-not-biased-against-women-at-work-read -this/#32ad57fd7e5a.

8. David Maxfield, Joseph Grenny, and Chase McMillan, "Emotional Inequality: Solutions for Women in the Workplace," *VitalSmarts* (n.d.), www.vitalsmarts.no/uploads/9/4/6/7/9467257/women-in-the-workplace -ebook.pdf.

9. Laura Montgomery, "How to Overcome Hidden Biases and Give Valuable Feedback," *The Economist* (n.d.), https://execed.economist.com /blog/industry-trends/how-overcome-hidden-biases-and-give-valuable -feedback.

10. Shawn Achor, "Do Women's Networking Events Move the Needle on Equality?" *Harvard Business Review* (February 2018), https://hbr.org /2018/02/do-womens-networking-events-move-the-needle-on-equality.

Chapter 7

1. Sylvia Ann Hewlett and Carolyn Buck Luce, "Extreme Jobs: The Dangerous Allure of the 70-Hour Workweek," *Harvard Business Review* (December 2006), https://hbr.org/2006/12/extreme-jobs-the-dangerous -allure-of-the-70-hour-workweek.

2. Tara Weiss, "How Extreme Is Your Job?" Forbes.com on NBCNews .com (February 18, 2007), www.nbcnews.com/id/17030672/ns/business -forbes_com/t/how-extreme-your-job/#.W7LvXRNKhSw.

3. Jena McGregor, "Millennial Women Aren't Taking the Vacations They've Earned," *Washington Post* (May 25, 2017), www.washingtonpost .com/news/on-leadership/wp/2017/05/25/millennial-women-arent-taking -the-vacations-theyve-earned/?noredirect=on&utm_term=.ca732d7c27c5.

The Business Case for Change

1. Ines Wichert, "The Business Case for Gender Balance," IBM Smarter Workforce Institute (2014), https://public.dhe.ibm.com/common /ssi/ecm/lo/en/lol14011usen/LOL14011USEN.PDF.

2. Sangeeta Badal, "The Business Benefits of Gender Diversity," *Gallup* (January 20, 2014), www.gallup.com/businessjournal/166220/business -benefits-gender-diversity.aspx.

3. Jonathan Woetzel and others, "How Advancing Women's Equality Can Add $12 Trillion to Global Growth."

4. Catalyst, *The Bottom Line.*

5. Samantha C. Paustian-Underdahl, Lisa Slattery Walker, and David J. Woehr, "Gender and Perceptions of Leadership Effectiveness: A Meta-Analysis of Contextual Moderators," *Journal of Applied Psychology* 99, no. 6 (2014): 1129–1145, http://dx.doi.org/10.1037/a0036751; Lee McNally, "5 Real Benefits of Gender Diversity in the Workplace" (March 5, 2015), www.linkedin.com/pulse/5-real-benefits-gender-diversity-workplace-lee-mcnally; Kevin Erdman, "Deepening the Talent Pool by Promoting Women's Leadership," Progressive Women's Leadership (August 27, 2015), www.progressivewomensleadership.com/deepening-talent-pool-womens-leadership/.

6. Josh Bersin, "Why Diversity and Inclusion Will Be a Top Priority for 2016," *Forbes* (December 7, 2015), www.forbes.com/sites/joshbersin/2015/12/06/why-diversity-and-inclusion-will-be-a-top-priority-for-2016/#4d9614762ed5.

Acknowledgments

I have tremendous gratitude for all who have inspired my writing and research, those who helped bring this incredible project to the finish line, and those who cheered me on over the years when I needed you most.

To the strong, smart, and bold women of my family who had the greatest impact on my life: my mother, Diane Snyder; my godmother, Patty Webb-Horst; my sister, Jaime Snyder; my cousins Margaret McCarthy and Maureen Niesborella; my mother-in-law, Rena Kuhl; and my sister-in-law, Dana LaPorta. And to my dad, Doug Snyder; my grandfather, Clarence Webb; and my father-in-law, Bill Kuhl, who never waver in their love and support for their daughters and granddaughters.

To my husband, Alex, who is a true partner in every aspect of our lives. You won me over with your elaborate home-cooked meals, but your work ethic, your compassion, your rock-solid support for both of our dreams, and the unbelievable father and role model you are to our girls give me more joy than I could ever imagine possible.

It was a blessing that my book proposal made its way to the hands of Neal Maillet, my editor at Berrett-Koehler, who ignited the fire inside me to see this vision through to its fullest. Danielle Goodman is hands-down the most talented, committed, and sincere developmental editor on this planet; she helped me unleash my voice. All the BK staff and community members who gave me energy at my Author's Day and through their role in this arduous process: Jeevan Sivasubramanian, Lasell Whipple, Sohayla Farman, Kristen Frantz, Chloe Wong, Mike Crowley, Susan Geraghty, Katie Sheehan, Johanna Vondeling, María Jesús Aguiló, David Marshall, Katie Sheehan, and Jennifer Kahnweiler (author of *The Introverted Leader*).

To the incredible team members who have made an impact since the inception of Why Millennials Matter. Florence Lee, you always find a way to bring my grand ideas to life through your talented and thoughtful design work. Caroline An, Matt Dubin, Brielle Jones, Allison Palacios, Gen Ste. Marie, Brianna Mercado, Vivian Peng, and Denise Chan: Your talents and contributions elevated the impact of our work to levels I couldn't accomplish without you. Wendy Yalom, Elsa Isaac, and Dayna Spitz, and Michelle Goldblum, Alison Leipzig, and Hillary Weiss of Soul Creative have empowered me in our pursuit to help more women have the confidence and courage to stay and slay!

I am thrilled to share throughout this book the stories of women I admire and who have filled my bucket with inspiration and willpower: Sandra Altine, Amanda Apodaca, Susan Axelrod, Zoe Baris, Theresa Batiller, Ashley Batson, Michelle Carnahan, Stephanie Epstein, Frances Hesselbein, Heather

Jackson, Laurie Kowalevsky, Kate Leiser, Carolyn Buck Luce, Chelsea Mohler, Vartika Prasad, Col. Diane Ryan, Jen Schubach, Kristen Shea, Tiffaine Stephens, and Laura Vang.

Female friendships are crucial in life, and I know how much these women have loved and supported me across significant moments in mine, so I am incredibly appreciative: Bekah Klipper, Denise Mondazzi Kane, Joy Robins, Carlene Greenidge (who is an incredible source of love and support to me and our entire family), Nikki Barker, Jen Haggerty, Nicole Lust, Elaina Filauro, Christian Nguyen, Holly Lindvall, Courtney McAlea, Dr. Nicole Nevadunsky, Rachael Toonder, Melissa Crandall, and Melanie Fried Walker.

To all of the courageous young women, leaders, and volunteers I have met through Girls Inc. of NYC, Girls Hope of Pittsburgh, Girls on the Run NYC, Step Up Women's Network, Girls Leadership, Girl Scouts of the USA, and the fellows (both women and men) of the Hesselbein Global Academy for Student Leadership and Civic Engagement at the University of Pittsburgh.

To my University of Pittsburgh (Pitt) family over the years, who never stopped cheering me on: Eva Tansky Blum, Cindi Roth, Sam and Anne Zacharias, Bob and Maryjean Lovett, Keith Schaefer, former chancellor Mark Nordenberg, Audrey Murrell, Lisa Cherok, and Liz Adams.

I am fortunate to have found many mentors and role models who gave me the energy and runway to go after my big dreams. It's my mission to ensure that more young women have this positive energy and bottomless support throughout their lives so that they too can dig their heels in. So, finally, thank you to the women who are leading and volunteering in organizations and groups that serve one another within corporations, communities, churches and other religious institutions, and schools. You are heroes, and the world would not be the same without you.

Index

About the Author

Photo by Wendy Yalom

Joan Kuhl, founder of the Why Millennials Matter and Courage to Stay movements, is an author, speaker, and unabashed champion of women and girls in leadership. Through her international speaking engagements, research, and consulting she's directly impacted on leaders from more than sixty countries and has transformed the internal workings of some of the world's largest corporations and institutions, including Goldman Sachs, Eli Lilly and Company, Johnson & Johnson, Moody's, Discovery Communications, FINRA, Novo Nordisk, Viacom, the NY Mets, and Columbia Business School. She spent thirteen years working in the pharmaceutical industry.

Over the years Joan has also made it her mission to directly support established and rising women leaders by launching and working with more than a dozen corporate women's networks and intergenerational employee resource groups, as well stepping into a role as a #SheBelieves Champion for the US Soccer Organization, becoming a contributor to Forbes-Women, and serving on the boards for the Frances Hessel-bein Leadership Institute and Girls Inc. of New York City. Her expertise has been featured in the *New York Times, Harvard Business Review,* CNBC, and *Success Magazine.* Joan is the author of *Misunderstood Millennial Talent: The Other 91%* and coauthor of *Peter Drucker's Five Most Important Questions: Enduring Wisdom for Today's Leaders.* Joan earned her BS/BA at the University of Pittsburgh and earned an MBA from Rutgers University, where she studied global business strategies in Beijing and Shanghai, China.

For more from Joan and updates on her latest empowerment and advancement initiatives (or just life with her two awesome, strong daughters), drop by www.joankuhl.com or say hi to her on Instagram at @JoanKuhl and LinkedIn: www.linkedin.com/in/joankuhl/.

Dear Ambitious Woman,

You may not know it yet, but your challenges in the corporate world are actually an opportunity in disguise to get what you deserve from your career and your organization while changing the lives of every woman within it—from the inside out.

My name is Joan Kuhl. I'm an author, speaker, researcher, and advocate for corporate equality, and if you're considering ditching your corporate job *you're not alone.*

It's no mystery why women are leaving the world's largest companies in droves.

Systemic gender inequality at every turn. From the pay gap to the struggle to get your voice heard, you often feel overlooked and undervalued.	The sixty-plus-hour work weeks, constantly being on call because you feel you must *have it all together* all the time to get noticed (and promoted).	The exhausting game that pits you directly against the boys club as you struggle to climb the ladder while others zipline it right to the top.	The constant tightrope walk of balancing motherhood with being a high performer, always sacrificing something.

It's enough to make you want to turn in your two weeks notice tomorrow, right?

But what if I told you there's a way to create a well-compensated, meaningful, happy, fulfilling career . . . by staying right where you are?

I'm on a mission to empower women everywhere with the tools, language, and confidence they need to dig their heels in and demand the change they deserve from within the corporate world. The next six pages in this book provide exercises and reflection questions to help you create a vision for your career and take action steps toward achieving it.

It all starts here with the courage to stay.

www.joankuhl.com

In Chapter 3: Setting the Stage for Success, I describe the importance of visualizing the career you desire. Evaluating the skill differences between your current role and your new one will help you focus on what can help you accelerate.

MIND THE GAP

Point A: Describe your current role

Point B: Describe the role you want

What four skills can help you cover the gap?

☆ _____

☆ _____

☆ _____

☆ _____

PLAY TO YOUR STRENGTHS

Point A: Describe your current strengths

Point B: Describe how your strengths could help you in the role you want

Describe a time your strengths helped you lead

In Chapter 6: Relationships Are Everything, we explore the various types of relationships that you must cultivate to truly thrive, not just survive, as you advance in your career journey. When possible, take the initiative to shadow someone who has the role you want or one that could expand your current skill set.

MENTOR MEETUP GUIDE

Mission: Ask your chosen mentor to share more about his or her responsibilities and the team he or she leads

- Can you describe your top priorities in this role?

- What are your individual goals for the year? What are your team's goals?

Processes: Describe the crucial processes that help you execute the demands of your role

- What systems do you use most frequently?

- What procedures did you have to learn for this role?

Team dynamics: Describe the members of your team and how they work together

- How often do you meet as a group?

- How do you structure your 1:1 meetings and how often do they occur?

- How do you approach recognition and development?

The support: Who else is important to these processes outside your team?

- What other stakeholders depend on your team's success?

- How does human resources support you?

- Do you have any mentors or peers whom you lean on for support?

Introducing yourself at a team meeting or at a networking event is an important opportunity to make a strong impression. Explore these questions to help you uncover more dynamic attributes to share so you can stand out.

TELLING A COMPELLING STORY

Your mission: What motivates you?

_____

_____

_____

_____

_____

Your passions

• What inspires you?

• What subject are you curious to learn more about?

Be memorable

- What skills do you wish others could know and appreciate about you?

_____

_____

_____

_____

_____

- Is there a defining attribute that captures who you really are today?

_____

_____

_____

_____

_____

Your career journey: What has been unique about your path thus far?

Berrett–Koehler
Publishers

Berrett-Koehler is an independent publisher dedicated to an ambitious mission: *Connecting people and ideas to create a world that works for all.*

Our publications span many formats, including print, digital, audio, and video. We also offer online resources, training, and gatherings. And we will continue expanding our products and services to advance our mission.

We believe that the solutions to the world's problems will come from all of us, working at all levels: in our society, in our organizations, and in our own lives. Our publications and resources offer pathways to creating a more just, equitable, and sustainable society. They help people make their organizations more humane, democratic, diverse, and effective (and we don't think there's any contradiction there). And they guide people in creating positive change in their own lives and aligning their personal practices with their aspirations for a better world.

And we strive to practice what we preach through what we call "The BK Way." At the core of this approach is *stewardship,* a deep sense of responsibility to administer the company for the benefit of all of our stakeholder groups, including authors, customers, employees, investors, service providers, sales partners, and the communities and environment around us. Everything we do is built around stewardship and our other core values of *quality, partnership, inclusion,* and *sustainability.*

This is why Berrett-Koehler is the first book publishing company to be both a B Corporation (a rigorous certification) and a benefit corporation (a for-profit legal status), which together require us to adhere to the highest standards for corporate, social, and environmental performance. And it is why we have instituted many pioneering practices (which you can learn about at www.bkconnection.com), including the Berrett-Koehler Constitution, the Bill of Rights and Responsibilities for BK Authors, and our unique Author Days.

We are grateful to our readers, authors, and other friends who are supporting our mission. We ask you to share with us examples of how BK publications and resources are making a difference in your lives, organizations, and communities at www.bkconnection.com/impact.

Dear reader,

Thank you for picking up this book and welcome to the worldwide BK community! You're joining a special group of people who have come together to create positive change in their lives, organizations, and communities.

What's BK all about?

Our mission is to connect people and ideas to create a world that works for all.

Why? Our communities, organizations, and lives get bogged down by old paradigms of self-interest, exclusion, hierarchy, and privilege. But we believe that can change. That's why we seek the leading experts on these challenges—and share their actionable ideas with you.

A welcome gift

To help you get started, we'd like to offer you a **free copy** of one of our bestselling ebooks:

www.bkconnection.com/welcome

When you claim your **free ebook**, you'll also be subscribed to our blog.

Our freshest insights

Access the best new tools and ideas for leaders at all levels on our blog at ideas.bkconnection.com.

Sincerely,

Your friends at Berrett-Koehler